**Sonya Hale, Jo**

# Glory Whispers

Bloomsbury Methuen Drama
An imprint of Bloomsbury Publishing Plc

B L O O M S B U R Y
LONDON • OXFORD • NEW YORK • NEW DELHI • SYDNEY

**Bloomsbury Methuen Drama**

An imprint of Bloomsbury Publishing Plc

Imprint previously known as Methuen Drama

| 50 Bedford Square | 1385 Broadway |
| London | New York |
| WC1B 3DP | NY 10018 |
| UK | USA |

**www.bloomsbury.com**

**BLOOMSBURY, METHUEN DRAMA and the Diana logo are trademarks of Bloomsbury Publishing Plc**

First published 2017

*Glory Whispers* © by Sonya Hale

*The Monkey* © by John Stanley

**British Library Cataloguing-in-Publication Data**

A catalogue record for this book is available from the British Library.

ISBN: PB: 978-1-4742-3245-6
ePDF: 978-1-4742-3247-0
ePub: 978-1-4742-3246-3

**Library of Congress Cataloging-in-Publication Data**

A catalog record for this book is available from the Library of Congress

Series: Modern Plays

Cover Design: Louise Dugdale

Cover images: top © tacojim/iStock, bottom © SensorSpot/ Getty images

Typeset by Mark Heslington Ltd, Scarborough, North Yorkshire
Printed and bound in Great Britain

To find out more about our authors and books visit *www.bloomsbury.com*. Here you will find extracts, author interviews, details of forthcoming events and the option to sign up for our *newsletters*.

**synergy**
Theatre Project

**Synergy Theatre Project** creates ground-breaking work which harnesses the energy, instincts and life experiences of those we work with – prisoners, ex-prisoners, young offenders and young people at risk of offending – gives them a voice and, in doing so, their dignity back. We inspire change by affecting feelings, attitudes and behaviour and provide practical opportunities which build a bridge from prison to social reintegration.

We are also concerned with the impact of our work on the public and use stories to humanise and provide new insights into the criminal justice system. Central to our approach is a commitment to artistic quality and empowerment of beneficiaries with the work taking place both in theatres and prisons and non-traditional venues, playing to diverse audiences and promoting mutual exchange between performers and audience to break down social barriers.

www.synergytheatreproject.co.uk

Company no: 4219146 Registered Charity: 1088692

# THEATRE503

**Theatre503 is the award-winning home of ground-breaking plays**

Led by Artistic Director Lisa Spirling, Theatre503 is a flagship new writing venue committed to producing bold, brave new plays. We are the smallest theatre in the world to win an Olivier award and we offer more opportunities to new writers than any other theatre in the UK.

## THEATRE503 TEAM

| | |
|---|---|
| *Artistic Director* | Lisa Spirling |
| *Executive Director* | Andrew Shepherd |
| *Producer* | Jessica Campbell |
| *Literary Manager* | Steve Harper |
| *Literary Coordinators* | Lauretta Barrow, Nika Obydzinski |
| *Operations Manager* | Anna De Freitas |
| *Marketing Coordinator* | Rebecca Usher |
| *Resident Assistant Producers* | Shae Rooke, Laura Sedgwick |
| *Office Intern* | Kay Benson |
| *Senior Readers* | Kate Brower, Rob Young |

## THEATRE503 BOARD

Royce Bell, Peter Benson, Chris Campbell, Kay Ellen Consolver, Ben Hall, Dennis Kelly, Eleanor Lloyd, Marcus Markou, Geraldine Sharpe-Newton, Jack Tilbury, Erica Whyman (Chair), Roy Williams.

## THEATRE503 HEROES

These brilliant volunteers give their valuable time and expertise to Theatre503 as front of house and box office managers, script readers and much more.

Alice Mason, Anna Middlemass, Anna Mors, Anna Landi, Andrei Vornicu, Asha Osborne, Annabel Pemberton, Bethany Doherty, Brett Westwell, Carla Grauls, Carla Kingham, Cecilia Garcia, Cecily King, Chelsey Gillard, Charlotte Mulliner, Chidi Chukwu, Damian Robertson, Danielle Wilson, David Benedictus, Dominic Jones, Elena Valentine, Emma Brand, Fabienne Gould, George Linfield, Gillian Greer, Imogen Robertson, Isla Coulter, James Hansen, Jim

Mannering, Joanna Lallay, Joe Ackerman, Joel Ormsby, Kate Brower, Kelly Agredo, Ken Hawes, Larner Taylor, Lisa Cagnacci, Lucy Atkins, Maddy Ryle, Mandy Nicholls, Mark Doherty, Martin Edwards, Michelle Sewell, Mike McGarry, Nathalie Czarnecki, Nick Cheesman, Nicole Marie Bartlett, Paul Webb, Rahim Dhanji, Rebecca Latham, Reetu Sood, Rob Ellis, Saul Reid, Serafina Cusack, Sevan Greene, Simon Mander, Stephanie de Whalley, Stuart Quinn, Tamsin Irwin, Tess Hardy, Tim Bano, Tobias Chapple, Tom Hartwell, Tom Latter, Tommo Fowler, Valeria Bello, Valeria Montesano, Vanessa Garcia, Will Callaghan, Yasmeen Arden.

## THEATRE503 IS SUPPORTED BY

Angela Hyde-Courtney, Cas Donald, Francesca Ortona, Georgia Oetker, Geraldine Sharpe-Newton, Gregory Dunlop, Katherine Malcom, Philip and Chris Carne, Stephanie Knauf, Sumintra Latchman.

## SUPPORT THEATRE503

Help us take risks on new writers and produce the plays that other theatres can't, or won't. Together we can discover the writers of tomorrow and make some of the most exciting theatre in the country. With memberships ranging from £23 to £1003 you can get involved no matter what your budget, to help us remain 'arguably the most important theatre in Britain today' (Guardian).

Benefits range from priority notice of our work and news, access to sold out shows, ticket deals, and opportunities to peek into rehearsals. Visit theatre503.com or call 020 7978 7040 for more details.

## VOLUNTEER WITH US

There are many ways to get involved in Theatre503, from joining our reading team to assisting during technical weeks or working front of house. If you're interested in volunteering please email volunteer@theatre503.com

Theatre503, 503 Battersea Park Rd, London SW11 3BW

**020 7978 7040 | theatre503.com**

The voices of prisoners and ex-prisoners are central to Synergy's work and through new writing we are excited to be able to broadcast those voices into contemporary British theatre. Sonya Hale and John Stanley found their way to Synergy because they had been through the criminal justice system and their plays give us empathy and insight into the diverse worlds that they have witnessed whilst showing that people are emphatically so much more than the crimes they committed. I hope that their success in getting their plays on to the professional stage will inspire other prisoners and ex-prisoners to pick up a pen because they make our theatre a more diverse and richer place for it.

Esther Baker
Artistic Director, Synergy Theatre Project


I wrote *Glory Whispers* when I was early in recovery from heroin and crack cocaine addiction.

During my addiction I became street homeless, ended up in prison and generally ran around like the characters in the play. However, it wasn't until my son was taken off me and went to live with his dad that it all became too much and I just couldn't cope any more with the pain of how I was living. I believe that it is this pain that got me into recovery and also is the drive behind my writing of this play.

I know many women who are caught up in a web of addiction and crime and destructive relationships with no idea how to live let alone bring up a child. I feel strongly that these women's stories need to be told.

Sonya Hale

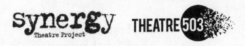

Synergy Theatre Project in association with Theatre503

# Glory Whispers

## By Sonya Hale

*Glory Whispers* was first performed at Theatre503
on 21 February 2017.

**Cast**

| | |
|---|---|
| **Mina** | Franc Ashman |
| **Glory** | Rachel Finnegan |
| **Jonno** | Dominic McHale |

| | |
|---|---|
| *Director* | Juliet Knight |
| *Designer* | Katy McPhee |
| *Costume Designer* | Emmett de Monterey |
| *Lighting Designer* | Rob Youngson |
| *Sound Designer* | Rebecca Smith |
| *Casting Director* | Nadine Rennie CDG |
| *Production Manager* | Steve Wald |
| *Stage Manager* | Holly Ellis |
| *Assistant Stage Manager* | Ronel Thomas |
| *Assistant* | Carrie Rock |
| *Fight Director* | Cristian Cardenas |

Please note that the text of the play which appears in this volume may be changed during the rehearsal process and appear in a slightly altered form in performance.

Supported by

 CALOUSTE GULBENKIAN
FOUNDATION
UK BRANCH

Sonya Hale

# Glory Whispers

**Mina**, *a large bubbly woman in her mid-forties but looks older, weathered, like she's smoked a lot and most certainly drunk too much. She has a burn on her neck that she covers with a silk scarf but it's still slightly visible. She wears a dressing gown over a tracksuit. She is overweight. Black. South Manchester accent.*

**Glory**, *a skinny woman in her late twenties. She is beautiful and, although she looks disheveled, she has a certain sex appeal. She is wearing an old tracksuit. She has a coat on that's too big for her and has hospital slippers on her feet. Her hair is wet and straggly. Northern accent with a hint of the London ting.*

**Jonno**, *a slender man in his late thirties–early forties. White. Skinny. Scruffy. He looks a bit like Adam Ant in a tracksuit. He has a feather in his hair. He looks like he needs a good hot dinner. He tries to talk in a gruff manly voice. He has a broad Wakefield Yorkshire accent.*

*A small, low-lit dingy flat in a high-rise block on a Penge Estate.*

*It's close to Christmas.*

*The room is cluttered with cardboard boxes, stacked on top of each other all around the edges of the living room, neat cardboard boxes. The room is shabby yet immaculately clean, like someone's tried to make the best out of not a lot. It's well ordered. An old sofa with an old crocheted throw on it faces the audience and a non-matching armchair faces the TV. The TV is on but the lights are off. It's gloomy. Laughter can be heard from the TV, a daytime chat show. The TV faces the sofa and chair. It's 'open plan' but small and cramped. The kitchen is adjoined to the rear of the living room, one door leads to the bathroom/bedroom area and one door leads directly onto the street. A balcony faces the audience to the left of the stage. The balcony curtains are closed. The walls are bare except for one picture in an old frame and a cracked mirror. The picture is of a bird flying over a sunset, it's tatty but neatly hung. The mirror has recently been smashed and a few shards of glass litter the carpet below along with a broken mug. A few well-fingered postcards of British seaside resorts are on the sideboard. Magazines are neatly laid out on the coffee table, like someone has tried to make the room look as 'a living room should look'. A big, spotty Royal Doulton teapot and tea set is on the table. The boxes, stacked against the walls, are tightly closed. It's claustrophobic.*

**Mina** *sits on the sofa. She has a dust cloth in her hand. She gets up. She dusts the teapot lovingly, wiping its rim, repeatedly. After a short while the kettle boils as* **Mina** *looks to the tea set with four cups. She picks up a cup, she sets it back down neatly, she shifts all the cups in the set into their correct place and arranges the other cups. She arranges them back how they were originally. The broken glass catches her attention. She goes to the kitchen. She gets out an old mug off the kitchen drainer and makes herself a cup of tea. She walks over to the balcony curtains with her cup of tea, it's steaming. She holds it to her lips but does not drink.*

*Pause.*

*She looks to the tea set. She looks away. Standing well back she looks through a crack in the curtains. She blows on her cup of tea and takes a small sip.*

*Beat.*

*She looks at the door.*

*Beat.*

*She looks at the tea set.*

*Beat.*

*She looks back out of the window. She looks, oblivious to the sounds of the TV. Her eyes fall to the floor . . . She closes her eyes. Suddenly she sets her cup of tea on the table. She grabs a dustpan and brush from the kitchen and sweeps up the broken mirror. She cuts herself . . .*

**Mina**   Fuck it!

*She looks at the cut. It's bleeding. She sucks it briefly.*

**Mina**   Fucking ouch . . .

*She carries on sweeping.*

*After a moment there is a loud bang at the door.* **Mina** *freezes. She stands with the dustpan full of glass and broken mug and looks around urgently for somewhere to put it. Another loud bang at the door.*

**Mina** (*Whispers.*)   Not now . . .

**Mina** *goes to open one of the boxes, thinks twice, goes to another one, thinks again.*

*Loud bang.*

**Mina** *tips the glass behind one of the boxes. The letter box opens. A voice whispers through the letter box.*

**Glory**   Pssst! Jonno . . .

*Beat.*

**Glory**   Oi. Psst . . . Jonno . . .

*Beat.*

**Glory**   Jonno. Psssssst. For fuck's sake, open up.

**Mina**   Shit.

**Glory** (*Voice louder, not heard* **Mina**.)   Oi! You prick.

**Mina** (*Bit louder.*)   Bugger off, there's no one here!

**Glory** (*The letter box closes – again not heard* **Mina**.)   Fuck's sake . . .

**Mina**   I suggest you get away from that door right now or else –

*Very loud bang at the door.*

**Glory** (*Shouted.*)   OI! Jonno! Jonno y' bastard! Open up! (*Bangs.*)

**Mina** (*To self.*)   It's not . . .

**Glory** (*To self. Whispered.*)   Be there you cunt, please be in . . .

**Mina**   Oh my god it's not . . . It bloody well is!

**Glory** (*Shouts.*)   Jonno!

**Mina** *puts down her cup of tea. She heads towards the door.*

**Mina**   Glory? Glory, my sweetheart.

*Beat.*

*Realises the TV is on. Turns it off. Checks the room.*

**Mina**   Glory! That you? Oh my god. Glory, my love!

*Straightens herself up and tucks her tummy in.*

**Mina**   Is that really you?

*She rushes to the door. She opens it.*

**Glory**   Mina.

**Mina**   Oh my gosh. How utterly lovely. It is you. It's really you!

**Glory**   Shit. Gosh. Hello . . .

**Mina**   I have missed you. Whispering like that y' funny bugger . . . Come here, y' daft sod, gimme a hug. (**Mina** *hugs* **Glory**.) Drove me stark stir crazy it has. I mean, I knew you'd be fine, don't get me wrong, didn't stop me thinking, though. (*Laugh.*) Look like you've seen a ghost, It's me, y' daft sod. (*Laugh. Brief beat.*)

**Glory**   It's bin a frickin' aeon.

**Mina**   Too long –

**Glory**   Yeah.

**Mina**   This is great. Amazing.

**Glory**   Wasn't sure you'd be in . . . I mean, I hoped, I did hope.

**Mina**   Two months now, me, out. (*Kisses the air.*) Suckling the nipple of freedom. Word travels fast though, in't it? I mean – Love you to think, to think to come. (*Beat. Laugh.*) What the hell happened? You look a bloody state, you're dripping wet and . . .

**Glory** *stands at the door looking wet and bedraggled.*

**Glory**  Thanks.

**Mina**  Well . . . Y' bloody do.

**Glory**  It's raining . . . I was in a rush, to see you, innit?

**Mina**  Agh! What me like? Come in, come in, sit down.
We're not bloody haunted! (*Fluffs up cushion on the sofa for*
**Glory**.) Look at that. How's that for cosy? Can't beat a bit of
that. Come on, come in, sit down. Sit.

**Glory** *enters the flat. She carries a Tesco's bag. She hesitates.*

**Mina**  I'll pop that there kettle on and . . . Y' dappy
sausage.

**Glory** *sits on the sofa.*

**Mina**  Tea? Tea. Or Coffee? Coffee perhaps? (*Goes to put kettle*
*on.*) And biscuits. Must have bickies, in't it, eh? Bourbons.
Chocolate Hob Nobs or . . . might even have . . . Taste the
Difference lemon cheesecake. I don't forget. I don't forget do
I Glory? You and your hungry tum always yammin'.

**Glory**  Got any smokes?

**Mina**  Glory . . .

**Glory**  Please.

**Mina** (*Beat. She hands* **Glory** *a packet of cheap fags.*)  Have us a
good old natter and . . .

**Glory** *takes an ashtray and sets it on the arm of the chair.* **Mina**
*watches.* **Glory** *lights her fag.*

**Mina**  And use an ashtray for goodness sake!

**Glory**  Jesus Min'.

**Mina**  You're not a tramp.

**Glory**  Sorry, alright?

**Mina**   No. It's me. It's me. I'm sorry. What ma like?
(*Laugh.*) Forget ma head if – (*Shouting behind her she heads off
to the kitchen to put the kettle on.*) What'll it be? Tea? Coffee? Got
the posh stuff. We're getting swanky. None of your freeze-
dried crap now. Café-frickin'-tierre, I tell ya. Funny I know
but . . . You want one of them? Giz ya reet buzz.

**Glory**   Don't fuss, I don't want fuss –

**Mina**   It's not fuss, awkward bugger. I'm making one
anyway. Tea. Milk, two sugar. See?

**Glory**   You got owt stronger?

**Mina** (*Shouts from the kitchen.*)   It's all very great getting
Spanish and fancy . . . coffee I ask y', but me and you –
Twisted PG. Sisters, innit? Could be arma-fricking-geddon,
the sky could crack and crash and suck out all the air and
we'd still say teaf one off the monkey love, donnez-moi un
cuppa, innit, eh?

**Glory**   Min'.

**Mina**   Stick the old goggler on. 'Nation's favourite blanket',
that tele, (*laughs, rummaging on the sofa.*) that's what they
reckon . . . (*She can't find the remote.*) Where's that bloody
remote? (*Laughs.*) Can't ever find it . . .

**Glory**   Mina –

**Mina**   Any-flipping-where. I have to find it –

**Glory**   Mina. Min.

**Mina**   Seriously now, it's fine.

**Glory**   Mina, just chill!

*Beat.*

**Mina**   Sorry.

**Glory**   No, it's me, I'm on edge, innit?

**Mina** *laughs.*

**Glory**    You got a proper drink and –

**Mina**    No.

**Glory**    Mina . . .

**Mina**    I said no.

**Glory**    I'm freezing my tits off like stalag-fucking-mites.

**Mina**    Glory, no. I can't believe you'd suggest –

**Glory**    It's one drink, warm us cockles.

**Mina**    I don't drink and nor should you.

**Glory**    Chance'd be a fine thing.

**Mina**    And he's reigned it in n'all. Proper got it under nibs . . . You think I'm knitting one . . . (*Laugh.*) Straight up! No messing! (*She is making the tea and shouts from kitchen.*)

*Beat.*

**Glory**    Where is J?

**Mina**    Out

**Glory**    Yeah?

**Mina**    Shops . . . got ever so good like that, these days . . .

**Glory**    What shops? When's he back?

**Mina**    The fucking shops, he popped out! I don't bloody know! Why you so bothered for him for?

**Glory**    I want quality time with you.

**Mina**    He'll go mental, bust a gasket if he finds you here.

**Glory**    I'll have words.

**Mina**    You?

**Glory**    Why not? A quiet word. He knows nowt could come between me and ma Mina. Say I just burst my way in.

**Mina** (*Beat.*)    Oh Glory.

**Glory**   He'll be sweet. One quick little tipple, proper sneaky like, before he gets back.

**Mina**   It's ten o'clock in the morning, Glory.

**Glory**   You boring fucking bastard! It's Christmas, Mina celebrate. Me and you . . . Get cosy . . . Av ourselves a 'Melted moment'. Innit?

*Beat.*

**Mina**   One drink.

**Glory**   Oh Min', you are electric, fetch us a merry England, I'll pay you back and get the munch in, I'm Marvin's, I would go myself but . . .

**Mina**   I'm not going shops.

**Glory**   I can't go like this. (*Gestures to self.*) Like you said, state of it.

**Mina**   Borrow some bits.

**Glory**   I don't wanna borrow bits. Can't you just go?

**Mina**   I won't get owt embarrassing.

**Glory**   I don't care what I look like, I can't face it.

**Mina**   Y' look like a drowned rat. And them shoes, what's with them, Glory?

**Glory**   I was in a rush . . . Excited, to see you, innit?

**Mina**   I'll fetch you something nice and warm and snug. (*Goes to get a jumper. Shouting from the other room.*) It'll probably be a dorky mind, by your standards anyway. (*Shouts from the next room.*) I've been meaning to step out of my comfort zone, try something new but . . . It's no fun shopping on me toddly, on me little Jackie old Jones, I get a bit . . . I dunno. (*She comes back in with jumpers and shakes them out.*) I tried on a dress at home last week, some internet horror, got it through the post – it was bloody traumatic! I looked like a big fluffy blancmange, a pig, all pink and wobbly. But with you, Glory

. . . Different . . . Ooooh . . . (*Excitedly holds up jumper.*) Look. Here. Try this.

**Glory**  Mina . . .

**Mina**  Or this?

**Glory**  Mina.

**Mina**  Ok then this?

**Glory**  Mina, I –

**Mina**  Just fucking take it! (*Beat.*) It's junk, I know it's junk.

**Glory**  Can't *you* just go?

**Mina**  He'll be back any minute.

**Glory**  So?

**Mina**  If he thinks you drew attention to the gaff he'll . . .

*Beat.*

**Glory**  He'll what?

**Mina**  Nothing.

**Glory**  Is he serving up?

**Mina**  No.

**Glory**  No?

**Mina**  No!

*Beat.*

**Glory**  If I put this on will you go to the shops, Min'?

**Mina**  –

**Glory**  For ickle me, Minny . . . (*Beat. Takes the jumper off* **Mina**.)

**Mina**  For god's sake . . .

**Glory** (*Taking her own top off she reveals her body in just a bra. She is very pale and very skinny. Laughs.*)   J needs t' get over himself. Remember the Scotch bonnet chillies? Absolute pisser! Me and you, sneaking in after a long night at it, 6am, to find him in the living room . . . Stark bollock knackers – pants round his knees, porn blasting . . . Well how could we resist innit? What did he expect? We only rubbed a couple in 'chilly chilly spicy hot willy Jonno!' Never seen a man so livid. Twat, lightweight! Thought he was gonna explode. Him crying and we falling about laughing so fricking much I . . .

**Mina** *falls silent and stares. Beat.*

**Glory**   What?

**Mina**   –

**Glory**   Fuck's sake, Min', spit it out!

**Mina**   I didn't say nothing.

**Glory**   Y' didn't bloody have to! Y' know what I'm like when I'm stressed. Might eat, might sleep, but I just can't store it. Y' know I loves me scram like but –

**Mina**   What've you got to be stressed about?

**Glory**   It's hard graft, you know that, I've been rushed off my feet.

**Mina**   You have to stay healthy, look after yourself, eat lots of wholegrain an' that.

**Glory**   I know.

**Mina**   Steak pie and chips.

**Glory**   Oh yeah?

**Mina**   I'll rustle you up a feasty.

**Glory**   Nice . . . Steak pie 'n' chips, with chip-shop chips?

**Mina**   With chip-shop chips. Big, fat, greasy mother of sin ones . . .

**Glory**   Wholegrain?

**Mina**   Ish . . .

**Glory**   Oh Min', you are a diamond. Grab some, when you go to the offie.

**Mina**   I'm not going to the shops, Glory.

**Glory**   But . . .

**Mina**   I'll cook for you but –

**Glory**   Fuck's sake, what is wrong with you?

*Beat.*

**Mina**   I was going to say if you keep a lid I'll check the cupboard – for a tipple, but if you're gonna be like that!

**Glory**   I'm sorry, Mina.

**Mina**   –

**Glory**   Min'? (*Smile.*) I'm sorry . . .

*Beat.*

**Mina** (*Goes into the kitchen and looks in a cupboard.*)   It's J's and for emergency use only. Understand? It's not mine!

**Glory**   Mina.

**Mina** (*Shouts from kitchen.*)   I don't. It's his, medicinal, it's occasional, just every now and then.

**Glory**   Thank you.

**Mina** (*Returns with a bottle of Grey Goose vodka.*)   Feast your clappers on that! Grey Goose, the finest!

**Mina** *hands it to* **Glory**. **Glory** *takes it.*

**Mina**   But please, just have a sup.

**Glory**   Ok!

**Mina**   It's his Goose L'orange collapso, Glory.

**Glory** (*Laughs.*)    Oh my gosh he's such a prick! I'll go easy, I promise, love him! (*Undoes vodka, sniffs it.*) Mmmm . . . Yummy . . . Thought you were gonna go chip shop . . . Get chip-shop chips?

**Mina**    You tranna get rid of me?

**Glory**    No.

**Mina**    Like y' got a wasps nest up ya.

**Glory**    I'm fine. I . . . I've missed ya. (*Laugh.*)

**Mina**    And I've missed you too but I can't, I swore down, promised I'd be in when he gets back and –

**Glory**    You promised *him* . . .

**Mina**    Says he's got . . . A surprise.

**Glory**    Oh yeah? (**Glory** *drinks.*)

**Mina**    Go easy, for god's sake, Glory. And use a glass will ya please? I told you, you're not a tramp!

**Glory**    A surprise?

**Mina**    Yeah.

**Glory**    Nice. (*Beat.*) Get us a glass then.

**Mina** *sighs and goes to get a glass from the kitchen.*

**Glory** (*Shouts to* **Mina** *in the kitchen and takes sneaky guzzles from bottle whilst she speaks without* **Mina** *noticing.*)    I appreciate this, Mina, really I do, something bloomin' chronic. I mean, when I say. Just special occasions and treats and that's like nigh on never. Straight up. Rare like beef, hardly ever drinking. Takes a lotta will power that, well, you should know but . . . it is worth it . . . it's worth it for me and . . .

**Mina** *returns with the glass.*

**Glory**    Responsibilities now innit, Min'? (**Mina** *gives* **Glory** *the glass and* **Glory** *starts to pour a drink.*) I mean . . . It's been

tough . . . don't get me wrong . . . a little bit craggy . . . rocky
. . . but, life ain't no fricking Alton Towers int it, Min'? Can't
expect to ride the log flume home. Hey? But now we're
diddling! Innit? Mina? Me an' you. Schdiddlywap! Whoa.
Schwing! (*Barrington Levy lyrics. Laughs.*) Run me down!
Diddly whoa!!! Diddly! (*She toasts* **Mina**.) Mina Schwing!
(*Laughs.* **Mina** *does not toast. Beat.*) What?

*Beat.*

**Mina**    Rocky?

**Glory**    Well not rocky, more like a pebble dash.

**Mina**    Fucking rocky?

**Glory** (*Tut.*)    Shut up.

**Mina**    You'd tell me if something w's up?

**Glory**    Yes. Nothing's up. We're fine. Buzzing . . . I just
need t' kick back, relax, which is why it's so damn good to be
here with you . . . I just ain't had time t' breathe.

**Mina** *hands her the glass.*

*Beat.*

**Glory**    For god's sake just have a bloody drink.

**Mina**    No.

**Glory**    Stop being weird.

**Mina**    I'm not being weird.

**Glory**    I feel like a freak on my own, you just sat there.

*Beat.*

**Mina**    Glory, no.

**Glory**    Let me . . . (*Gestures* **Mina**'s *feet.*)

**Mina**    What? No.

**Glory**    The old dead kippers . . .

**Mina**    Oh you're mad, you are.

**Glory**    Cough 'em up,

**Mina**    Never! They're mank!

**Glory** (*Wiggles her toes out of the hospital shoes.*)    Let 'em join the par'e! One of a kind. Ain't none got the touch like –

**Mina** (*Takes socks off to expose her rotten feet. She puts her feet on the table.*)    Look. See. Told ya – Mank! (*Wiggles her toes.*)

**Glory** (*Looks at feet.*)    Jesus, Min . . .

**Mina**    I did warn you.

**Glory**    I know but . . . (*She goes to touch her feet then does a pretend gag.*)

**Mina**    If you're gonna be like that!

*She goes to take her feet off the table.*

**Glory**    Joke! I was joking . . . Give 'em here . . .

**Mina** *puts her feet up. Beat.* **Glory** *goes to massage them.*

**Mina**    That tickles . . .

**Glory**    Sorry . . .

**Mina**    No, nice tickle, not  . . .

**Glory**    If you want I –

**Mina**    No it's fine, it's lovely. Please don't stop I . . . (*Beat.*) It's lovely.

**Glory** *continues to massage* **Mina**'s *feet. Beat.*

**Mina**    I've missed you. (*Laugh.*)

**Glory**    And I've missed you too.

**Mina**    Really?

**Glory**    Yes of course.

**Mina**    Yeah?

**Glory**    Yes! I said yes, didn't I? Look, don't start.

**Mina**    I ain't heard from you f' god knows how long. Tried to track you down, soon as I got out. Searchin' the internet –

**Glory**    Things have been hectic.

**Mina**    Nearly three years!

**Glory**    –

**Mina**    Where y' bin living?

**Glory**    Peckham. Got a flat.

**Mina**    That's nice.

**Glory**    Yes, it is.

*Beat.*

**Glory**    Proper –

**Mina**    Not far then?

**Glory**    Look, I've had a lot on. I thought about you, 'course I did, constant, but before I knew it days became weeks became months and . . . Keeping the show on the road . . . You know what it's like . . . I'm here now, int a Min'?

*Beat.*

**Glory**    Min'? (*Beat.*) Oh my days, look at chew . . . My god I've missed ya!

*Beat.*

**Mina** (*Suddenly jumps up.*) (*Stands up, stands in front of the balcony curtains.*)    Fuck him. Fuck him and his 'keep them curtains shut, Mina' . . . 'Prying eyes . . .' my gaping umchawada! We've got nothing to hide! He's an idiot. You're here now after far too long and I for one am going to make the most of it. (*She throws the balcony curtains open. Dust flies around the room. They haven't been opened for a long time. She* *stands and looks out with the curtains open. She breathes.*) Look at it. Fucking glorious!

*She looks out off the balcony and breathes like she's seeing it for the first time.*

**Glory**   Mina . . .

**Mina**   Check it out!

**Glory**   Must ya Min'?

**Mina**   Y' can see The Shard from my balcony . . . I said they should call it the broken –

**Glory**   Very scenic I'm sure –

**Mina**   Bloody well is, yeah . . . Just have t' squint y' eyes a little and tilt y' head t' the left and imagine . . . Make like it's . . . (*Beat.*) You remember . . .? (*Laugh.*) Tesco's roof . . . What a pisser! Clambering up after a hard night at it. Like monkeys . . . I'd nigh break ma neck but you . . . (*Gasp.*) You! You'd scamper off like a little chimp. And we'd stand up there. (*Sings Barrington Levy Here I come.*) 'Shiddlywoahaha ahiddly diddly woah . . .' (*Shouts off balcony.*) Take that y' bastards! Lobbing up chips at the cunts. And that you seedy bugger! Yes you. Have that with your chippy spunk gravy! (*Laugh.*) . . . Spark me a fiver and expect me to swallow, Bastard. (*Sings.*) 'Diddly woah! Diddly woah! Diddly woah, schwing!' Fucking . . . Glory! Come and have a schwing with me!

**Glory**   Mina –

**Mina**   Come!

*Beat.*

**Mina**   All the plans you had, all the places you were going to go like you'd bonked Sir David Attenborough and out popped a travel brochure. (*Laughs.*) You made it alright, Glory, you took it all away. (*She holds out her hand to* **Glory**. **Glory** *does not take it.*) That you upped and left I'm ok with. You did what you had to do. But . . . Come and have a look at ma shard with me, come check out ma broken –

**Glory** *does not move.*

**Mina**    I got your postcards. (*Grabs one of the cards off the TV and shows it to* **Glory**.) Denmark. Belgium. Amsterdam. (*Beat.*) Paris. Romantic, look, I bet?

**Glory**    Oh my god, you kept them?

**Mina**    You must be bursting with stories to tell?

**Glory**    Yeah.

**Mina**    Outright gonna pop!

**Glory**    Yeah . . . Mina.

**Mina** (*Points at postcard of Eiffel Tower.*)    I mean, check that out f' a gaff!

**Glory**    Mina . . .

**Mina**    Fucking what?

**Glory**    Where's J?

**Mina**    Shops, I said, bloody shops.

*Beat.*

**Glory**    So what's with the boxes?

**Mina**    Nothing.

**Glory**    You moving out?

**Mina**    Don't be daft. No, as if. (*Beat.*) It's just bloody boxes, innit?

**Glory**    It's like –

**Mina**    Just leave it.

**Glory**    Min' come on –

**Mina**    It's storage. Just bits, stuff, old . . . Your poems. You want me to show you?

**Glory**    My poems?

**Mina**  Yes. Your bloody poems and Post-it notes.

**Glory**  No!

**Mina**  Great hoarded boxes of it, bursting at the seams –

**Glory**  You fucking kept 'em?

**Mina**  Yes. Of course.

**Glory**  Oh my god!

**Mina**  Boxes and boxes of 'em. Look.

**Glory**  No!

**Mina**  Oh you are silly . . .

**Glory**  I don't wanna –

**Mina** (*Quotes a poem.*)  'Together we can hitch the stars, Together ride the moon, Stick us tits out, Shake us leg and tick, tick, tick, boom!' (*Laughs.*)

**Glory**  Fuck's sake.

**Mina**  And another . . . 'For you I pledge eternal, for you I love you so . . .'

**Glory**  Y' know 'em by heart?

**Mina**  Yes. ' . . . For you I dance the cows come home, for you I let me go.' Beauty.

**Glory**  Bullshit.

**Mina**  Poetry! Come an' hav' a look at me shard.

**Glory**  No. (*Glugs on vodka.*)

**Mina** (*Stands at window. Beat.*)  Glory?

**Glory**  It's just the fucking Shard, I know what it looks like!

*Beat.*

**Glory**  Look, I'm sorry it's just –

**Mina**  J says I've got every right to be angry with you, says if we never spoke again it's a moment too soon . . . I mean, I told him I'm not, angry that is, it's not about grudges, we love you, end ov. But with him . . .

**Glory** *swigs on vodka.*

**Mina**  It's adoption week.

**Glory**  What?

**Mina**  Saw it on tele earlier. Made me feel ever so gank. Had 'em all lined up, young-uns on *This Morning*, one after the other, you'd think it was pet rescue. Or lonely hearts, or . . . One after the other. They were all 'This is Roger, he's four and this is Josh, he's six. Like I'm at the checkout. Bleep. Joshua. Bleep. Roger. Bleep . . . Paul, bleep and then . . . 'This is little Emma, a wee babby. Six months, and I lost it. I went ballistic! And any fuckin' psycho can bag one these days! Just 'On special offer' down the shopping channel. Even that Jolie's bagging another. Everywhere everyone's baggin and bagsyin and blagging 'em and I just wanna . . . I exploded! I fucking lost it. I couldn't see, couldn't think, I couldn't stop t'. Glory, I hope you're grateful and cherishing each second coz . . . I smashed the fucking mirror. (*She gestures a cracked mirror on the wall.*) Look at that. I don't know what came over me. See?

*Beat.*

**Mina**  T' think . . . Little old me . . . (*Laugh.*)

*Beat.*

**Glory**  Mina, it's ok.

**Mina**  Get me all in a frenzy . . . (*Laugh. Beat. Grabs a postcard of the Eiffel Tower off the tele.*) But 'Bon-fucking-jour!' Bet you can't beat the view from the top of the Eiffel Tower, eh?

*Beat.*

**Glory**   I didn't go up.

**Mina**   Didn't go up? Le Tour d'Eiffel but –

**Glory**   Got scared.

**Mina**   You?

**Glory**   No not me, him . . . Vertigo, innit?

**Mina**   He's scared of heights?

**Glory**   That is vertigo.

**Mina**   But –

**Glory**   His little legs shaking . . .

**Mina**   I bet he looks like you, innit?

**Glory**   A bit . . .

**Mina**   Handsome, got your eyes . . . What is it – watch out neighbourhood, watch out girls, here comes a king?

**Glory**   He's 2½, Min'.

**Mina**   2½ . . .

**Glory**   But growing up fast.

**Mina**   I want to meet him.

**Glory**   And you will.

**Muggy** (*Shouting from street below. He carries a can of Special Brew, his dog is running around off the lead and he's obviously very drunk.*)   Oi Oi!!!

*Beat.*

**Muggy** (*Whistle.*)   Oi! Mina! (*Whistle. Dog bark.*) Shh. Fuck's sake shut up. (*Woof.*) Mina! (*Dog bark.*) Shut up!

**Mina**   Bloody little pest . . .

**Glory**   Is that . . .?

**Mina**   Yeah.

*Beat.*

**Muggy** Oi! Fucking Mina!

**Mina** (*Goes to look off balcony.*) Keep your bloody voice down, Muggy.

**Muggy** Alright Min', wass up?

**Mina** I said keep your voice down. What do you want?

**Muggy** J sent me.

**Mina** Did he, love? (*Gestures him to keep quiet.*)

**Muggy** Yeah, said t' say he –

**Mina** That's nice.

**Muggy** What?

**Mina** That's lovely sweetie. Perfect. How's your Sharon?

**Muggy** (*Confused.*) He said t' say –

**Mina** She alright?

**Muggy** Yeah. I er . . .

**Mina** She had it yet?

**Muggy** What?

**Mina** Bigger than an Arctic truck she was and I said Oooh . . . that's gonna hurt you gally, your gonna need more than an epidural f' that one.

**Muggy** She ain't pregnant.

**Mina** What?

**Muggy** She's not pregnant, listen Min' –

**Mina** Oh, y' joking . . . (*Laugh.*) Hear that, Glory? What a boobie! Oopsy.

*Beat.*

**Mina** Glory?

**Glory** *is hiding from the window.*

**Mina**   Glory what's wrong?

**Muggy**   Mina!

**Mina** (*Shouts.*)   Shut up!

**Muggy**   He just wanted to say he's stopped off, picking sommat up on his way home, but that he's on his way –

**Mina**   Thanks love. Got ya, take care.

**Muggy**   But . . .

**Mina**   And feed that bloody dog of yours! (*To* **Glory**.) What's going on?

**Muggy** *leaves. Beat.*

. . . Well?

**Glory**   What?

**Mina**   Why you hiding from him for?

**Glory**   I'm not.

**Mina**   Really?

**Glory**   No.

**Mina**   Not what it looks like – (*Shuts the balcony window.*)

**Glory**   He's a first-rate cock, Min', a blithering idiot –

**Mina**   It's Muggy . . .

**Glory**   I don't wanna get sucked back in.

**Mina**   Y' not in the bloody *Godfather*, Glory!

*Beat.*

**Mina**   So are ya?

**Glory**   What?

**Mina**   Hiding something?

**Glory**   No.

*Beat.*

**Mina**   So why won't you let me meet him? You could bring him round?

**Glory**   No way!

**Mina**   Why not?

**Glory**   Because of tossbags like him. Bad news . . .

**Mina** *suddenly snatches* **Glory**'*s Tesco bag.*

**Glory**   Mina!

*They wrestle with the bag.*

**Glory**   Mina, Give it me back! Min' . . . Get off . . . it wouldn't be safe to bring him round –

**Mina** *grabs it away from* **Glory**.

**Glory**   You're bang out of order, you are!

**Mina**   And you're like a slippery snake, we're supposed to be tighter than . . . (*She looks inside the bag. Beat.*) Oh my . . . Oh my goodness . . . (**Mina** *reaches into the bag pulls out a bundle of jonnies.*)

**Glory**   Happy now?

**Mina**   Oh my Glory days, what in hell\s name are you doing with . . .

**Glory** (*Snatches the bag off* **Mina**.)

**Mina**   You're not . . .

**Glory**   No.

**Mina**   Is it the money?

**Glory**   No. I'm not!

**Mina**   Glory!

**Glory**   Shut up y' fool . . . I got the horn.

**Mina**   The horn?

**Glory**   Yes.

**Mina**   There's an awful lot.

**Glory**   I'm awful fucking horny! (*Beat.*) Look, I've got these neighbours, dead nice they are, had a party. Met this girl, dead civilised it was.

**Mina**   What the hell you need them for if you met a girl?

**Glory**   No she . . . She's proper caring.

**Mina**   Oh yeah?

**Glory**   Childminder, like. Registered and everything. Gets me a cheap deal –

**Mina**   So that's where he is?

**Glory**   Yes.

**Mina**   Don't trust me, is that it?

**Glory**   What? No! Mina . . . Don't be silly –

**Mina**   Me! It's been 2 years, nearly 3. You didn't even send me a photie in prison!

**Glory**   Yes I did.

**Mina**   No you didn't! You bloody well didn't, Glory. Just . . . Postcards, empty . . . (*Reads card.*) 'Hi Min', having a great time, wish you were here, thinking of you, love and hugs.' What the hell is that?

**Glory**   A postcard.

**Mina**   It's like you don't even know me –

**Glory**   Shut up.

**Mina**   You used to write deep, you used to write poetry.

**Glory**   I did wish you were here.

**Mina**   Well it don't bloody sound like it. That . . . That's shit! I sat up night after night alone in that cell, grasping on to the hope that . . . J's got more depth than you!

**Glory**   J?

**Mina**   More romance, more poetry.

*Beat.* **Mina** *grabs bottle of vodka and goes to the kitchen.*

**Mina**   Maybe this was a mistake.

**Glory**   J wouldn't know romance if you spiked it up his japsi.

**Mina**   He got me this. (*Shows her a limp-looking spider plant.*)

**Glory**   J, y' galliant bastard!

**Mina**   Shut up.

**Glory**   Shit a sunbeam . . . (*She takes the plant and lifts one of its wilting leaves.*)

**Mina**   It was beautiful when he got it me.

**Glory**   Oh yeah, really?

**Mina**   Smelt like spring.

**Glory**   Spring is it?

**Mina**   So I over-did it with the water a bit . . .

**Glory**   Do ya think?

*Beat.*

**Mina**   So it's a tad wilty . . .

**Glory**   Wilty ain't the word, Min! It's J's alright.

**Mina**   You're bloody rude you are.

**Glory**   Wilty wilty . . . (*Laugh.*) Look, Min. I've been thinking . . . me and you, later, Tesco's roof, innit? Cadge ourselves a landscape? I still got tha poet . . .

**Mina** *shuts the balcony curtains.*

**Mina**   You can't get close any more. They fenced it off, barb wire. Like the flippin' Helman Province now it is.

*Pause.*

**Glory**   He's lovely you know, Mina.

**Mina**   Yeah?

**Glory**   Proper magic. Bright, blazing, blue star eyes and freckles all over that scatter him. Strawberry blonde hair, soft and curly that y' can't stop sniffing. He's bright *and* he's funny, have you in stitches. Got a double cow's lick and he thought, right, honestly, cows come in the night and lick him. How sweet is that?

**Mina**   Sweet.

**Glory**   I say his freckles are where fairies bin dancing.

**Mina**   –

**Glory**   Drives him mental.

**Mina**   He'll sprout wings next. Watch out y' don't find him pissing through a halo up Regent's Park or something.

**Glory**   Fuck up . . . (*Beat. Tries to laugh.*) That's his dad. (*Beat.*) Shit, Min', come on . . . I ain't seen the cunt in timage, not since I had –

**Mina**   Why won't you let me see him?

**Glory**   Karli?

**Mina**   Yes, flipping Karli! (*Beat.*) You think I'd upset him?

**Glory**   No. It's just . . .

*Pause.*

**Glory**   I'm sorry!

**Mina**   Yeah?

**Glory**  Really I am. I –

**Mina**  Really . . .

**Glory**  Yes. 'Course I flippin am. It must have been hell –

**Mina**  Do ya think?

**Glory**  I can't imagine.

**Mina**  No. Right.

*Beat.*

**Mina**  You really don't think it's safe, do you? You think I'm a risk?

**Glory**  No.

**Mina**  Cheek.

*Beat.*

**Glory**  I know about J.

**Mina**  What about J?

**Glory**  Serving up.

**Mina**  Don't be daft!

**Glory**  You're telling me he's not?

**Mina**  No. He's . . .

**Glory**  Not what I heard.

**Mina**  You heard wrong.

**Glory**  It's all over the grape vine.

**Mina**  What in hell's name are you doing on the grape vine?

**Glory**  People talk.

**Mina**  What people?

**Glory**  Filthy-Phil and Nice-but-dim –

**Mina**  What you chat to them for?

**Glory**   I don't. I bumped into them, outside cash
converters. They were skittin' about tranna flog a sat nav,
desperate to raise a score. On account that they owed you
money.

*Beat.*

**Mina**   Not me. J.

**Glory**   J's serving up smack and drinking and you're telling
me it's safe to bring Karli round?

**Mina**   Him, not me, I stayed clean!

**Glory**   Really? You lie to me about J . . .

**Mina**   I didn't want to upset you. I thought you wouldn't let
me see Karli if –

**Glory**   Too right I bloody wouldn't.

**Mina**   It's not me, Glory, I promise you, I won't have a bar
of that shit. I told J, point blank, no one comes round here,
not ever, not any more. If you're gonna serve up do it out on
street. (*Beat.*) You're drinking . . .

**Glory**   It's not even the same league. And hardly anyway
. . .

**Mina**   He's holding it down.

**Glory**   Serving up.

**Mina**   He's not using.

**Glory**   What the hell's he do it for then?

**Mina**   Stuff. Luxuries. I dunno.

**Glory**   What luxuries?

*Beat.*

**Mina**   He's got some mad hock idea.

**Glory**   Oh yeah?

**Mina**    You know what he's like.

**Glory** (*Laugh.*)    Where to this time?

**Mina**    Glory.

**Glory**    Where to?

**Mina**    He's got his little heart set on it. Ever since I got out he's not spoke about owt else.

**Glory**    Where's he taking you?

**Mina** (*Beat.*)

**Glory**    Go on.

*Beat.*

**Mina**    The Outer Hebrides.

**Glory**    The fucking Outer fucking Hebrides?

**Mina**    Yes.

**Glory**    You having a laugh?

**Mina**    No. He's deadly serious.

**Glory**    What y' wanna go there for?

**Mina**    Because it's stupendous! White sandy beaches . . . hill-tops, mountains, perched on Europe's cusp, he says. We're retracing his Braveheart roots.

**Glory**    He's from bloody Wakefield!

**Mina**    Not far . . .

**Glory**    And what you gonna do when you get there?

**Mina**    Be happy. I dunno. Settle or something. He's gonna be clean and I'll . . .

**Glory**    You'll what?

**Mina**    He needs to get away from it, Glory. Says we can't stop . . .

**Glory**  And what about you?

**Mina**  Me?

**Glory**  Yeah.

**Mina**  You have no idea –

**Glory**  All this madness . . . J serving up and you're telling me you ain't used or nothing?

**Mina**  Yes! How fricking dare you? How very fricking . . . I held on, white-knuckled it, not a drop or a . . . or a sniff the whole time I was in. Hard graft, Glory, believe. Some of what I had to put up with . . . My pad mate, Catherine, pretty little thing she was. Skin like milk, angelic and this big bright red auburn mane – stunning – I mean, god knows what she's doing in there. Tapped. (*She taps her head.*) Tunes of a loon. Jibbering and flapping round the wing like a lost bit of litter, every screw knew it . . . Everyone knew don't give her a lighter. This one time, I was stood in the meds queue all quiet and tidy eyes glued to the floor when suddenly boom! There she comes screaming and grasping full pelt, wailing and hollering, like a crazed banshee. Head full flame. Bright blue and orange flames there was, coming off her head and she's all 'Can you hear me fucking now, can y'? Can y' hear me fucking now?!!' Screaming, head t' toe she was. Guy Fawkes . . . Mate! And the screws? *Feckless tourists!* . . . Getting all in a fuss . . . One shot a water cannon. Straight at her face. Like she's flaming electrical goods. Skin flew everywhere, and hair. Splatterin' the walls and the ceiling. And Glory, the smell. Oh my god how it lingered. Screws got shrinked, we got locked behind our doors. Locked down with it like a bad bastard mist. The haunting, I called it. Back on the wing the other girls took the piss something vile. Shouting and tormenting. They called her Catherine wheel, Glory, imagine . . . I said not to give her a light. And me? They ghosted me . . . shipped me off to bloody *Timbuktu* or something, with no contact from anyone, en-y-one, no J, no nothing! I didn't know if he was dead or alive and . . .

Scratching my eyes out for 6 months, Glory, staring at blank walls, shitty little window overlooking another brick wall, concrete –

**Glory**   Fuck.

**Mina**   Yes, fuck.

**Glory**   *You* got ghosted?

**Mina**   I pissed myself in Lidl's last week, I thought this security feller was a screw, jangling his keys he was. The shock was that much, *that much* it shook me. It was hell on earth in there, Glory, literally, but I didn't use. Not once. (*Beat.*) And do you know what kept me going?

**Glory**   –

**Mina**   Do you know what got me through all that, Glory?

**Glory**   No.

**Mina**   This. (*Beat.*) This moment. I've had it planned for so long, Glory, going round and round my head like a washing machine . . . You'd be there at my door with a big grin on and no time for flowers . . . Just . . . We'd be nervous and fidget and I'd want to explode but I wait, we'd wait and . . . crack a smile, then boom! And we'd be hugging and hugging and probably crying even and kissing so hard he'd get squashed like a . . . Like a little Karli sandwich –

**Glory**   Mina, love ya –

**Mina**   That's what kept me going, Glory. That and you.

**Glory**   (*Takes a swig of vodka.*)

*Beat.*

**Glory**   For fuck's sake, Mina, I said I'm sorry, what else do you want?

**Glory** *takes another swig of vodka.*

*Pause.*

**Mina**   Why whisper Jonno through the letter box?

**Glory**   What?

**Mina**   You heard me.

**Glory**   To check he wasn't in.

**Mina**   Yeah?

**Glory**   Yes.

**Mina**   Do you want to know why I got ghosted?

**Glory**   What?

**Mina**   Well, do ya?

**Glory**   Ok –

**Mina**   I smashed some girl's face in the sink.

**Glory**   Yeah?

**Mina**   'Catherine wheel! Catherine wheel!' They were on, on and on at her, I couldn't bloody stand it, couldn't stand by and watch – so I grabbed this girl's head by the gruff of her neck and I kept smashing her and smashing it, blood – I mean, I don't know what came over me . . . Covered she was.

*Beat.*

**Glory**   Shit.

**Mina**   You owe me, Glory.

**Glory**   What?

**Mina**   You, fucking owe me.

**Glory**   You told me to go, insisted, put £50 quid in my hand.

**Mina**   Yes I did.

**Glory**   I was pregnant!

**Mina**   And y' never even sent a photie. (*Beat.*) You're not sorry.

**Glory**   Yes I am. 'Course I am. We were wild, all three of us, none of us fit t' . . .

**Mina**   None of us fit t'?

**Glory**   No!

**Mina**   Oh my gosh.

**Glory**   What?

**Mina**   Clear as day. I see it now.

**Glory**   Mina, no. Oh my god no, I'm so fucking sorry –

*Beat.*

**Mina**   It's me, isn't it?

**Glory**   What?

**Mina**   You think I'm scummy?

**Glory**   What? No.

**Mina**   You think I'm too scuzz and disgusting . . . too fucking wrong to –

**Glory**   No!

**Mina**   With your posh bloody trips, La Paris . . . I bet that bastard childminder's French even isn't it? Swanking off . . . Got new mates now is it?

**Glory**   No.

**Mina**   Leave your fat numpty sidekick. The only one who stuck by you. Would your new posh mates do time for you, Glory?

**Glory**   Time for me?

**Mina**   Yes, for you. You owe me Glory.

**Glory**   For fuck's sake!

*Beat.* **Mina** *snatches the vodka and takes it to the kitchen.*

**Glory**   Mina! (*Follows* **Mina** *to the kitchen.*)

**Mina** *puts on rubber gloves and starts scrubbing.*

**Glory**   Mina, come on . . .

**Mina**   J was right about you all along . . .

**Glory**   What?

**Mina**   Flighty little skanky . . . Think of no one else but . . .

**Glory**   Min' . . .

**Mina**   I need to make J's brecky. Black pudding, sausages, beans and –

**Glory**   I've had a lot going on.

**Mina**   Yeah?

**Glory**   Big stuff.

**Mina**   Me too! Funny that, eh?

*Beat.*

**Glory**   I went to see my mum.

**Mina**   I'm sorry?

**Glory**   My mum, she –

**Mina**   What the fuck in hell did you go and do that for?

**Glory**   She's sick . . .

**Mina**   She's bad news!

**Glory**   Proper.

**Mina**   We said never go back, we promised.

**Glory**   I know but . . .

**Mina**   What you tranna do?

**Glory**   It's spread.

**Mina**   Good!

**Glory**  To her heart, to her lungs, she's in a wheelchair now.

**Mina**  Still manage to demolish the offie I bet?

**Glory**  . . . Yeah, but she looks just dead . . . old and tiny.

**Mina**  She still with him?

*Beat.*

**Glory**  Yeah.

**Mina**  And you still merrily went to visit?

**Glory**  She's riddled.

**Mina**  You're crazy! What were you thinking? Huh?

**Glory**  She'll always be my mum, Min'.

*Beat.*

**Glory**  I was thinking . . .

**Mina**  What?

**Glory**  She's all I've got, I was thinking, and with her being ill 'n all.

**Mina**  She won't change, Glory.

**Glory**  You think I don't know that? You think I don't fucking . . . She's a cunt!

*Pause.*

**Mina**  Ok.

**Glory**  Even on the way up she's tranna scab me money . . .

*Beat.*

**Mina**  You daft bugger . . . You daft, daft fucking sod. You're too forgiving, Glory . . .

**Glory**  But –

*Moments pass . . .*

**Mina** *returns to scrubbing. Beat.*

**Glory**   I'll check.

**Mina**   What?

**Glory**   I can't promise anything but . . .

**Mina**   What?

**Glory**   Karli. I'll have t' check t' see if it's possible. No promises but I could have a word.

**Mina**   I'm sorry?

**Glory**   Like I say he's at the child minders.

**Mina**   You fucking what?

**Glory**   Straight up. They've got activities booked, I-flipping-tinery.

**Mina**   Oh my gosh, fuck, for real?

**Glory**   Yeah. Don't get excited.

**Mina**   I'm not! I could get a few bits in, it is Christmas. I could get a bird in, not a big one –

**Glory**   It's not –

**Mina**   Bread sauce . . . Or I could come to you, if y' still frets about J . . . Come stay at yours. I won't be bothering.

**Glory**   The house is a mess, Mina.

**Mina**   As if I give a hoots about that.

**Glory**   Like a bomb hit it, getting a new kitchen fitted. I ain't got an oven –

**Mina**   So bring him here. I'll send J to the pub, he'll be buzzing and we'll have the place to ourselves.

**Glory**   Maybe . . .

**Mina**   When?

**Glory**   What?

**Mina**   Sod Christmas. Let's get him now. Sneaky . . . Go grab him out of nursery. I really want to see him.

**Glory**   Mina . . .

**Mina**   When can we get him?

**Glory**   Later.

**Mina**   Today?

*Beat.*

**Glory**   Ok.

**Mina**   Oh my gosh, we both . . . Me and you . . . Get him from that minder's?

**Glory**   Yes.

**Mina**   Promise?

**Glory**   I said –

**Mina**   We could go now.

**Glory**   They've got activities.

**Mina**   It's a special occasion.

**Glory**   Ain't some hillbilly got him, you can't just waltz in.

**Mina**   Later though?

**Glory**   Yes.

**Mina**   Which one?

**Glory**   What?

**Mina**   The minder's?

**Glory**   'Tits and tots.'

**Mina**   'Tits and bloody tots?'

**Glory**   Yeah.

**Mina**   Tots? And tits? That's just rude, that is.

**Glory**   Look, Mina –

**Mina**   Where is it?

**Glory**   Beckenham.

**Mina**   What time? What time they finish?

**Glory**   Midday.

**Mina**   Fuck me. I'll need to get him a pressie, get it from Argos. What's it these days? Mario? J plays it 24/7.

**Glory**   No it's not.

**Mina**   It is!

**Glory**   He's 2.

**Mina**   Oh. Ok.

**Glory**   It's all about the pirates.

**Mina**   I knew that.

**Glory**   Jake and the Netherlands.

**Mina**   The Netherlands, my fave.

**Glory**   It's shite, Yankie bullshit.

**Mina**   But he loves it.

**Glory**   Yeah.

*Beat.*

**Glory**   D' y' know what it's about, Mina?

**Mina**   What?

**Glory**   Do ya? (*Jamaican accent.*) I say do you know what it's all about!?!

*Beat. Knowing look between* **Mina** *and* **Glory**.

**Mina**   What's it all about, Glory?

**Glory**   Me and ma pump um ting!

**Mina**   Glory.

**Glory** (*She starts to shake her ass.*)   Run me down! Woah!!!

**Mina**   You're pissed.

**Glory**   'Schuddidlly bop! Woahoaho . . .' (*Starts to sing 'Barrington Levy Here I Come'.*)

**Mina**   Wally.

**Glory**   So join me! (*Offers* **Mina** *the bottle but* **Mina** *doesn't take it.* **Glory** *takes a swig and dances, singing intro of 'Barrington Levi Here I Come'.*) '. . . Diddly, whoa, swing . . .' (*Etc.*)

**Mina**   Glory.

**Glory** (*Continues to sing.*)   'Because you are old and I am young . . . (*Grabs* **Mina** *to dance.* **Mina** *complies hesitantly at first.*) a*nd while I'm young yes I wanna have fun, run me down! Diddly woah whoa diddly diddly whoa . . .'

**Mina** *laughs.*

**Glory**   'Swing!' Now ya shaking ya pum pum ting!

**Mina** (*Laughing and shaking her bootie.*)   Shake a little battie at the boys, work it girly! Now I'm shaking ma pump pum.

**Glory** *and* **Mina**   Ting! (*Laugh.*)

**Mina**   'Over the ocean over the sea.'

**Glory**   'All of the girls dem a pose for we.'

**Mina** *dances silly and attempts to sing 'diddly woah' bit of the song but gets all tongue twisted. They fall about laughing.*

**Glory**   You are such a tit!

**Mina** *gasping for breath.*

**Both** *laughing.*

**Mina**   Oh fucking hell, Glory, I knew you'd see sense. I've missed you so goddam much.

**Glory**   Me too! (*Pushes* **Mina** *playfully.*) Fuck aye I've missed –

*The click of a key in the door.* **Mina** *and* **Glory** *freeze.* **Mina** *pushes* **Glory** *to hide in the kitchen.* **Glory** *hides. The key has clicked the door open. Brief beat.* **Jonno** *boots the door open with his foot. The door bursts open.* **Jonno** *enters with a bulky, tatty JD Sports holdall.*

**Jonno**   Raaaa!!! Freedom!!! Like Wallace himself popped out of ma chest! (*He stands in the doorway. Chucks holdall on living-room floor.*) I know I took a while but I couldn't resist. On me way home . . . I swiped you Scotland! Every little hillside, moorland, seaside cove . . . Like a Scottish Ninja, me. Little suity-booty sat behind his desk, didn't know what hit him. I looked him dead in the eye, one-a momentous stand off (*sings good, bad, ugly theme*). Then raaaa! I I swipe it. The entire fucking Northern Hemisphere, for you! (*Grabs bundle of Scottish holiday brochures out of the holdall to show* **Mina**.) Y' gotta check the Butt of Lewis, Min', fucking fantastic – craggy, windswept, proper rush-a-gush-in-your-fanny. If that don't squeeze your juice, Min', if that don't flick ya pea, I'm Princess Lily arse wipe in a fluffy pink dress. Thomas Cook . . . Sassenach Bastards.

*Throws off his coat. Moves the coffee table and swipes all the magazines and everything off the table in one swoop.*

**Mina**   Jonno . . .

**Jonno**   For fuck's sake! Scotland, innit? . . . I sorted it alright? (*He reaches down his trousers and from between his bum cheeks he reveals a parcel. He holds it and admires it.*) 50 teenths and ten half sixes, *on tick*. Who's your fucking warrior now, Min'? Who's your Wallace? (*Throws drugs on the table and his arms up in the air, quoting* Braveheart *film.*) 'He consumed the English with fire from his arse and lightning from his . . .' (*Thrusts his cock.*) Raaa! 'Freedom!!!'

**Mina**    J, for god's sake.

*Beat.*

**Jonno** (*Reaches into the ripped lining of his leather jacket and pulls out a little bunch of limp snowdrops. He hides them behind his back.*) As if I'd forget. (*He suddenly produces the flowers. He grins. They wilt.*)

**Jonno**    My merry dancer.

**Mina**    Thanks.

**Jonno**    Festive-ish.

**Mina**    I can see that, love.

**Jonno**    I'm yer Wallace.

**Glory**    Alright J? Still yannin' f' y' Scotland?

**Jonno**    What the fuck?

**Glory**    Like a lost Nessy and a mad wet blanket dream.

**Jonno**    What the fuck is she doing here? (*He closes the brochures and picks up the parcel.*)

**Glory**    Bit wilty, eh? (*Gesturing the flowers.*)

**Jonno**    What is she doing?

**Glory**    Scotland . . . Fancy . . . Min' said you were on some mad bloody crusade but –

**Jonno**    What the fuck is she doing?

**Glory**    Riding y' haggis to the holy land (*Mimics riding a horse.*) Clipperty clop. Clipperty clop.

**Jonno**    Get out.

**Mina**    Jonno . . .

**Glory**    Min' says she's just so excited.

**Jonno**    I mean it, get her out.

**Glory**   The Outer fucking Hebrides . . .

**Jonno**   Fucking out!

**Mina**   Jonno, please.

**Jonno**   Piss taking . . .

**Mina**   She's come all this way.

**Glory**   Yeah, Jonno –

**Mina**   You know what this means to me. We've just been chatting, catching up, nothing hectic.

**Glory**   Nowt hectic, Jonno.

**Jonno**   Nowt hectic?

**Mina**   It's been lovely. Sweet. I'm so excited, so happy I –

**Jonno** (*Roars.*)   Fucking Raaa!

**Glory**   Chill J . . . man, seckle . . .

**Mina**   It's Glory, J, she's . . . fam innit? (*Laugh.*) The three of us, since the dawn of bloody everything, she was so excited to see you . . .

**Glory**   Gallie's right, mate.

**Mina**   Could barely contain herself.

**Glory**   Och aye, no lie.

**Jonno**   Get out.

**Glory**   No.

**Jonno**   Don't push me.

**Glory**   Or what?

**Jonno**   Or what?

**Glory**   Or fucking what?

**Jonno**   I'll –

**Glory**    You'll do what, Jonno?

**Jonno** *glares.*

*Pause.*

**Glory**    Look Jonno, I ain't come to cause grief, just wanna see Min', rekindle . . .

**Mina**    And kindle a new . . .

**Jonno**    You what, kindle –?

**Mina**    Relations, Jonno . . . Kindle new –

**Jonno**    Kindle new relations? Sorry . . . What's going on?

**Glory**    Nothing's changed, Jonno. Just . . . catching up. Old times sake, innit?

**Jonno**    Catching the fuck up?

**Glory**    Yes. Yeah. Innit Min'?

**Mina**    Look what he got me, tranna palm it off as mistletoe, cheeky bugger tranna . . . (*Grabs snowdrops and holds them up.*) Hey, J, go on, catch me . . .

**Jonno** *glares.*

**Mina** (*Laughs.*)    Tell y' Glor' it's been that long –

**Glory**    I'll snog ya! (*Leaps up to give* **Mina** *a peck on the lips.*) Mmmm . . . Like licking the arse of a honey wet bee . . .

**Mina**    Without the sting.

**Glory**    Of course!

**Mina**    Just . . . Soft and furry . . .

*They laugh.*

**Jonno**    She's rat arsed.

**Mina**    So?

**Jonno**    Steam boats pissed.

**Glory**   Problem being . . .?

**Jonno**   You better not have given her . . .

**Mina**   What? No.

**Jonno**   Mina!

**Mina**   I told her she could have it, me, sorry J.

**Jonno**   My Grey Goose voddy? My VX – exceptionnelitie?

**Mina**   I'll get you another one.

**Jonno**   It cost a fortune!

**Glory**   There's still *some* left . . . (*Holds half-empty bottle of vodka out. Giggles.*)

**Jonno** (*Grabs it.*)   Give me that.

**Mina**   It's just vodka, Jonno.

**Jonno**   You drank half of it. (*To* **Mina**.) You were ragging her – cunting her off just last week.

**Mina**   J . . .

**Jonno**   Spitting feathers. Said not ever did you want to see her face again –

**Mina**   I did not.

**Jonno**   Yes. Y' did.

**Mina**   I was having a strop. (*Beat.*) So? (*Laughs.*) You two, bloody cheer up. Anyone would think . . . J, love, you've got half a bottle, I'll fetch you a glass. (*Beat.*) Sit . . . J, please . . . Glory . . .

**Glory** *sits.* **Jonno** *stays standing.* **Mina** *carefully removes the bottle from* J's *grasp and goes to the kitchen to pour him a glass.*

**Mina** (*Shouts through from kitchen.*)   No hoo har, J, promise, good as gold now, in't it, Glory?

**Glory**   Yup.

**Jonno** (*Whispers to* **Glory**.)   Kindle new relations?

**Mina** (*Shouting from kitchen.*)   Gonna cook up chips 'n' gravy J. Glory's be on and on about it. You two and your tummies . . . All you love me for, innit?

**Jonno**   New fucking relations?

**Mina** (*Reappears with a pint of vodka. Beat.*)   J, love, it's just a chat. (*Beat.*) Y' scare off wildcats looking like that, sit down y' egit.

**Jonno** *does not sit down.*

**Mina**   J, love, (*Tries to tempt with vodka.*) Y' collapso del bar excellantei . . . (*Beat.*) For god's sake we've all made mistakes. God only knows you made enough.

*Beat.*

**Jonno**   Fetch me a blade. (*Pulls the table towards himself so it's in between his knees. She puts the pint glass on the table. He moves the pint of vodka to the back left-hand corner of the table. He arranges the table so it's straight and puts the parcel in the middle of the table. He is neat, almost O.C.D. in his arrangements.*)

**Mina**   J . . .

**Jonno** (*Shouts.*)   Mina!

**Mina** *goes to the kitchen to fetch a blade.*

**Jonno**   What the hell are you playing at?

**Glory** (*Shouts to* **Min** *in the kitchen.*)   Scotland, Min', you excited?

**Mina**   What love?

**Jonno** (*To* **Glory**.)   I said what do you want?

**Glory**   Scotland, buzzin eh?

**Mina**   What? Yeah. Can't wait!

**Glory** (*Whispered to* **Jonno**.)   You even asked her if she wants to go?

**Jonno**   Yeah.

**Glory**   Really?

**Jonno**   What's it t' you?

**Glory**   William Wallace, ya Scottish heroic. Look at the state of it. (*Picks up brochure.*) She really gonna take to this? You think? She be lonely as sin. (*Flicks through the brochure.*) Bleak, deserted, windswept . . . Oh no, what we got here? Sheep, now that should clinch it.

**Jonno**   You so much as whiff the slightest hint of a breath of grief and I swear down I'll . . .

**Glory**   You'll what?

**Jonno**   I'll . . . (*Drinks vodka.*)

**Glory**   You can't say owt J.

**Jonno** (*Shouts.*)   Mina! Blade!

**Mina**   Alright! Steady on. Twisted knickers sweetheart.

**Jonno**   And fetch the bloody mirror.

**Glory** (*Whispers.*)   Things are criss with me and Min'. We chatted.

**Jonno**   You chatted? What the hell did you say?

**Glory** (*Shouts to* **Mina**.)   I was gonna fetch him on a visit.

**Mina**   Yeah?

**Glory**   Got as far as the prison gates . . . But no place for a nipper eh?

**Jonno** (*Whispers.*)   What are you doing?

**Mina**   That would have ruined me!

**Glory** (*Whispers.*)    Don't say squat then. (*Shouts.*) You know, I really am a good mum, Min.

**Mina**    I bet you are sweetie!

**Glory**    Like a fish to water really . . .

**Mina**    I always said, didn't I, J? Motherhood'd bring out the best 'n you, that's what I said. That you'd dash all this, proof's in the pudding, in't it?

**Glory**    Don't say squat.

**Jonno**    You'll break her heart.

**Mina**    Tad-aaa! (*Suddenly produces blade from the kitchen. Laughs.*) Play nice, you two. (*Hands blade to* **Jonno**.) Watch y'self love, it's ever s' sharp.

**Jonno** (*Drinks vodka.*)    And mirror. Mina. Mirror. It ain't gonna chop itself.

**Mina** (*Hesitates.*)    I . . .

**Jonno**    What?

**Mina**    . . . Smashed it . . . (*Laughs.*) Oops . . . (*Beat.*) Silly –

*They look at the mirror on the wall.*

I'm like the ugly sister. (*Laughs.*)

**Jonno**    I ain't having this, Min'.

**Mina**    It's not her, I did it before she got here, I just . . . I got upset . . . J. I'll clean it up. Before she arrived. (*She reaches behind one of the boxes.*)

**Jonno**    –

**Mina** (*Pulls out a bit of mirror.*)    Look, there's a bit, it's fine! I'll dust it.

**Mina** *wipes the mirror on her trousers and gives the mirror to J.*

**Jonno**    – (*He takes the mirror. He wipes it. He puts it down.*)

**Glory** *looks uncomfortable.*

**Jonno** *notices* **Glory**. *He unwraps the drugs. Watching* **Glory**.

*Beat.*

**Mina**   Can't you do it in the bedroom, love?

**Jonno**   No.

**Mina**   It's winding us up.

**Jonno** *growls.*

**Mina**   She's clean.

**Jonno**   Really?

**Mina**   Yeah. Like little knickers flapping . . . (*Laughs.*) In't it, Glory? You do her nut in. Must ya?

**Jonno** *picks the parcel up. He opens the knot in the top of the bag. He is aware of* **Glory** *watching him. Looks at* **Glory**. *Smiles. He slowly starts to empty the contents out onto the mirror.*

*Beat.*

**Jonno**   Yeah. I must.

**Glory** *jumps up to the balcony curtains. Hesitates.*

**Jonno**   What are you doing?

**Glory**   Letting the sun in.

**Jonno**   Yeah well –

**Glory** *throws open balcony curtains.*

**Jonno**   Fuckin' shut it!

**Glory**   Prying eyes . . . (*Giggles.*) (*She points off the balcony at a robin.*) Look at him! (*She glances back at J.*)

**Mina**   Oh my gosh! Little tyke . . .

**Glory**   He looks famished.

**Mina**   So sweet!

**Jonno**   Min', the window.

**Glory**   Got any bread?

**Mina**   I don't know –

**Jonno** (*Grabs* **Glory**, *shoves her back inside and slams the balcony door shut. He pushes her against the wall.*)   Do you want her to end up fucking back inside?

**Glory**   –

**Jonno**   Well? Do ya?

**Glory**   Don't be so –

*Beat.* **Glory** *meets* **Jonno**'s *glare. They glare. Beat.* **Jonno** *lets go of* **Glory**.

**Jonno** *shuts balcony curtain.*

**Glory**   She told me all about you . . . keeping her cooped up, like a caged bird.

**Jonno**   She ain't caged.

**Glory**   She ain't been out f' weeks. Don't *need* bloody tag with you –

**Jonno**   I don't keep her fucking caged! She sits in day after night after day watching shitty tele. Too scared t' . . . Too scared after . . .

**Mina**   That's not true J.

**Jonno**   Yes it is.

**Mina**   Box sets innit? *Game of Thrones.* (*Laugh.*) Bin telling us about y' travels, int ya love?

**Jonno**   Travels?

**Glory**   Yeah.

**Mina**   Got vertigo up the Eiffel Tower and what a lovely new gaff she's got and what with Karli –

**Jonno**   What?

**Mina**   She's gonna let me meet him.

**Jonno**   I'm fucking sorry, what?

**Mina**   I said bring him round f' Christmas but hardly appropriate, so I'm going to pick him up.

**Jonno**   Karli?

**Mina**   Yes, J. He's at the minder's, Beckenham.

**Jonno**   You're having me on.

**Mina**   I've waited a thousand Christmases, or 's what it feels like, J. I'll bring you a doggy bag . . .

**Jonno**   Sit the fuck down.

**Mina**   Jonno . . .

**Jonno**   Sit.

**Mina**   But . . .

**Glory**   Tweet tweet, Jonno. Caged bird sings.

**Mina**   . . . Argos, love . . . It's Christmas.

**Jonno** (*To* **Glory**.)   Just you try it.

**Glory**   You're jealous.

**Jonno**   Of what? Of you?

**Glory**   Of me and Min', us magic we got.

**Mina**   Oh, y' not love? Y' don't have t' be jealous.

**Jonno**   Listen Glory . . . There's three things I'm good at in life. Shagging, shotting and causing a –

**Glory**   Ruckus. Yeah, so y' say.

**Jonno**   If it's a ruckus you want, bring it fucking on.

**Glory** (*Beat.*)   Innit?

**Mina**   Please, you two!

**Jonno**   You've got nothing Glory.

**Mina**   J, love.

**Jonno**   Remember that. Nothing. Gone. Poof. (*Sits down to chop up drugs.*) If I were you I wouldn't push it.

**Glory**   I didn't come here to fight.

**Mina**   He knows that really, in his heart, innit it love, hey?

**Jonno**   Sit down.

**Glory**   You *both* would have loved Paris you know, J. I would have loved to take you.

**Mina**   You hear that love?

**Glory**   Nothing would a made me buzz more . . . Vineyards, Châteaux, frogs-legs –

**Mina**   Frogs legs?

**Glory**   And proper cheap vino, J, you woulda lapped it up like a dog, in your element . . . and the view from the Pompidou –

**Jonno**   Always filling her head with fancy shit stories –

**Mina**   J!

**Jonno**   Three bastard bin bags I filled with your shite. Filling her up and filling her up and she's so bastard gullible. Y' fucking post-it notes and shit poetry, I threw them out.

**Glory**   Mina?

**Mina**   I didn't know Glory, honest.

*Beat.*

**Glory**   So what's in the boxes then?

**Jonno**   Let it go Glory.

**Glory**   Just what is your problem?

**Jonno**  You want to know what's in the boxes?

**Mina**  No.

**Jonno**  You really wanna know?

**Mina**  J, don't.

**Glory**  Min', get yer coat.

**Mina**  What?

**Glory**  You ain't right J.

**Mina** *doesn't move.*

**Glory**  Get your coat!

**Mina** *jumps.*

**Jonno** (*To* **Mina**.)  You're going nowhere.

**Mina**  J, don't be daft. (*Goes to leave.*)

**Jonno** (*Grabs* **Mina** *violently.*)  You fucking stay where you are.

**Glory**  Jonno.

**Mina**  J –

**Jonno** *holds her. Beat.*

**Mina**  J, let go of me.

*Beat.*

**Mina**  Let go of me, please. (*Beat.*) You're better than this Jonno.

**Jonno** *lets her go.*

**Mina**  Let me get my coat. (*Leaves to get her coat.*)

**Jonno** (*Whispering to* **Glory**.)  What the hell are you playing at?

**Glory**  Jonno –

**Jonno**    You get there, then what?

**Glory**    I'll think of sommat.

**Jonno**    Midday? That's half an hour.

**Glory**    I'll tell her he's got a tummy bug, that she best get home.

**Jonno**    She won't buy that.

**Glory**    She will if I get a text message, from the 'minder'.

**Jonno**    She can't find out!

**Glory**    She won't. I'll make sure of it. She won't, she can't . . . (*Beat.*) Unless you tell her. (*Beat.*) And if she finds out you knew all along . . .

**Jonno**    She needs me.

**Glory**    Really?

**Jonno**    Yes.

**Glory** (*Laugh.*)    Her William Wallace? Her Tartan fucking pimpernel. Just, sort me out quick and I'll go. If I go now, quick, you can console her. You're good like that, I'll come back straight after, smooth it, she loves you, Jonno.

**Jonno**    I'm not giving you fuck all.

**Glory**    Jonno, please.

**Jonno**    No.

**Glory**    This is me, Jonno, me, Glory. You've always been there for me, I know that, I look up to you for god's sake, you're like my big brother. You saved my life. Neither of us would be alive if it wasn't for . . . You. (*Touches his face softly.*) Us versus the world, Jonno . . .

*Pause. She strokes his face.*

**Glory** *goes to kiss* **Jonno** . . .

**Jonno**    What the fuck are you doing? (*Grabs her hand.*)

**Glory**    Jonno.

**Jonno**    When you two first came to London. When you got off the bus, do you know what you said?

**Glory**    No.

**Jonno**    'We've come to nick your sunshine, y' bastard!' I remember it clear as day. And I never ever thought you would but y' have, y' did, y' nicked it.

**Mina** (*Shouting from the other room.*)    Two shakes of a fluffy little lamb's tail!

**Jonno**    Fuck you.

**Glory**    J please . . .

*Big clang.*

**Mina**    Agh!

**Glory**    What the hell happened to us?

**Jonno**    You. You're what happened.

**Glory**    Don't deny it Jonno.

**Mina**    I'm alright, I'm fine. Don't worry about me!

**Jonno** *glares at* **Glory**.

**Mina**    . . . Bastard boxes . . .

*Beat.*

**Jonno**    If I sort you out (*Grabs parcel off the table.*) you get the fuck . . . You get your arse in there and you tell her you've got a flight, booked, you're moving to Paris. You *and* Karli, it leaves soon. He's already at the airport waiting. You came to say goodbye, for good. This is Auf Wiedersehen, bonne chance . . .

**Glory**    Jonno!

**Jonno**    Get in there and say it.

**Glory**   But –

**Jonno**   Teenth of each t' pack y' bags and say that's it.

**Glory**   Jonno . . .

**Jonno**   Promise, you'll say it.

**Glory**   Just give me the gear –

**Jonno** (*Holds gear.*)   Say it.

**Glory**   But . . . It's Mina . . . For god's sake, Jonno, don't be a prick.

**Jonno** *dangles the drugs.*

**Glory**   Don't be an idiot.

*Beat.*

**Jonno** *withdraws the drugs.*

**Glory**   My mum, she's proper sick, I need Mina . . . I can't . . .

**Jonno** *returns to chopping drugs.*

**Glory**   I can't do it alone. I need her. She's like my . . . She's my everything.

**Jonno** *shrugs. Chopping drugs.*

**Glory**   For fuck's sake!

*Beat.*

**Glory**   Ok, Ok. I'll say it.

**Jonno**   Yeah.

**Glory**   Yeah.

*He puts the parcel in her hand. He holds her hand. They look each other in the eye. Beat.*

**Glory**   Jonno . . .

*Looks round and sees* **Mina** *stood at the door.*

**Jonno**   Just making peace, innit Glor'?

**Glory**   What? Yeah. Peace. (*Laugh.*) Man.

**Mina**   –

**Glory**   Sorry about all that, Min –

**Jonno**   Just . . . Like we've got some mad dysfunction innit but all good now. (*Drinks a big gulp of vodka.*)

**Glory** (*Laughs.*)   Screamin' and shoutin', what we like eh?

**Jonno** (*Puts his arm round* **Glory** *and grips her.*)   Love her really.

**Mina** (**Mina** *stands in the entrance to the room. She's carrying a little coat. It has fur round the collar.*)   I found your coat.

*Beat.*

**Mina**   You must have left it. Years ago. Gatherin' dust . . . (*Laughs.*) Ouchy, boxes fell on my head . . . (*Rubs her head. Beat.*) Go on then, take it. (*Offers the coat.*) We are going out J.

*Beat.*

**Mina**   . . . So if you need anything . . .

**Glory**   Ta . . . (*Takes the coat.*)

**Mina**   And bugger me blind, you're gonna need shoes Glory.

**Glory**   Mina . . .

**Mina**   . . . And hat and scarf, two mins maxi –

**Glory**   I –

**Mina** *goes to look for more clothes.*

**Glory** (*Whispers.*)   I can't do it.

**Jonno**   You have to.

**Mina** (*Shouts from down the hallway.*)   Chop fucking chop . . .

**Glory**   Not while I'm in bits. I'll say the wrong thing. I'll be much more compos mentis –

**Jonno**   No.

**Glory**   You watch my back, I'll do it here, in the khazi.

**Jonno**   Just fucking tell her.

**Glory**   I'll be dead quick . . .

**Jonno**   I've lost count of the amount of times I've risked it all for you, put my neck on the line while you scamper off, scot-free, laughing. Risking a kicking, again and again, punters, dealers, I've had enough, Glory, end of, fucking tell her.

**Glory**   Jonno, please.

**Jonno**   Not any more.

**Glory**   What about my mum?

**Jonno**   What about her?

**Mina** *appears at entrance to kitchen.*

**Mina**   Ready? (*She stands at the doorway wearing her coat and scarf and bobble hat and carrying a red beret.*)

*Beat.*

**Mina**   Well?

*Beat.*

**Mina**   Look what I found ya. (*Shows beret.*) Perfect, see? It's French. (*Puts it on.*) 'Bon-fucking-jour . . .' (*Beat.*) Half past eleven, can't leave him waiting. (*Beat.*) What's going on?

**Glory**   I . . .

**Mina**   What?

*Beat.*

**Glory**   Sit down.

**Jonno** *swigs vodka.*

**Mina**   Don't you bloody start.

**Glory**   Please, just sit.

**Jonno** *continues to swig his vodka more and more frequently throughout the following section.*

**Mina**   I don't want to.

**Glory**   For god's sake sit down!

**Mina** (*Sits down.*)   What's going on?

*Beat.*

**Mina**   Tell me.

**Glory**   He won't be at the gates.

**Mina**   Why not?

*Beat.*

**Glory**   He's sick.

**Mina**   What? Shit.

**Jonno**   Glory . . .

**Glory**   I didn't want to tell you, it's infectious, he's in quarantine.

**Mina**   Oh my gosh, did he get it in France?

**Glory**   No.

**Mina**   Y' get all sorts in France. Bloody rabies, all sorts –

**Jonno**   He's not got fucking rabies.

**Mina**   I do know that Jonno, I'm just saying.

**Glory**   He's got mumps.

**Mina**   Mumps? Love him!

**Jonno**   Glory!

**Mina**   So where is he then?

**Jonno**   Don't you dare.

**Glory**   He's in hozzy. Hospital, but he's fine he –

**Mina**   Oh my god! Hospital? With mumps?

**Jonno**   Just fucking tell her!

**Glory**   J.

**Mina**   Tell me what?

**Jonno**   Glory's planning a trip. Int ya Glory? A little escapade.

**Mina**   Escapade?

**Jonno**   Yes escapade. Me and you are gonna go to Scotland and Glory . . . Fucking tell her then!

**Glory**   Mina. Love. I've gotta go. Karli. You get me? It's been lovely to see you. I'll come back. Promise and we'll catch up proper.

**Jonno**   You ain't fucking –

**Mina**   Let me come!

**Glory**   No.

**Mina**   Is he very sick?

**Glory**   He's fine, it's just –

**Mina**   But hospital . . . Escapades . . . I don't understand.

**Glory**   He's ok. He's just upset. He needs me.

**Mina**   What's going on?

**Glory**   –

**Jonno**   Glory?

**Glory**   No. Min' it's fine.

**Jonno**   Just say it!

**Glory**   J, please, I need to get Karli. (*To* **Mina**.) Don't listen to him.

**Jonno**   You ain't going nowhere. Sit down.

**Glory**   Really Jonno I'd love to but . . .

**Jonno**   Stop feeding her hope, you cunt.

**Glory**   Jonno please . . .

**Glory** *grabs her coat and bag and goes to leave.*

**Jonno** *grabs her and pulls her back into the room.*

**Jonno**   You're fucking going nowhere till . . .

**Mina**   Jonno, please.

**Glory**   You're hurting me.

**Jonno**   Mina! (*To* **Glory**.) Let's have a little dance shall we?

*Beat.*

**Jonno** (*Canes the vodka, throws the bottle and flicks the stereo on. The Fratellis Whistle For The Choir starts playing.*)   Tune!

**Glory**   What?

**Jonno**   Oh yes . . .!!! (*Laughs and starts dancing.*)

**Glory**   You ain't right.

**Jonno**   Dance the hengandi frango! Av ourselves a fucking tango! (*Laughs and sings along to The Fratellis.*)

**Mina**   J, sweetheart . . .

**Jonno** (*He is dancing seductively and singing like a tit. Trying to get* **Glory** *to dance. Taunting and teasing her.*)   Merry little dancers. Aurora Borealis's each and every one of us!!! Bring it on! Whistle for the choir, Glory!

**Mina**   J, love, you ok?

**Jonno**   I'm braw bricht like a wee merry dancer.

**Glory**    I've got t' go.

**Jonno**    You ain't going nowhere. (*Swigging vodka.*) Dance! Wi' me!

**Glory** *grabs her stuff and goes to leave.*

**Jonno**    Sit down.

**Glory** *dashes for the door.*

**Jonno**    I said sit down! (*He grabs her and pushes her on the sofa.*)

**Mina**    Jonno.

**Jonno** *stands above* **Glory**, *panting.*

**Glory**    Holding us hostage? After everything . . . All that with my mum and . . . You're nothing but a coward Jonno. A pathetic coward. (**Jonno** *laughs.*) Call yourself a man? You really think you're some kinda something, don't cha? Look at you, all 'big man bwoy', 'gangsta' wid cha bare big wad of ping. Knob-head. Where were ya then Jonno? Me and Mina both out grafting –

**Jonno**    Want me to tell her?

**Glory**    Do me a favour.

**Jonno**    Want me to tell her about you and your spectacular fuck up?

**Mina** (*Switches the music off.*)    Someone please tell me what is going on!

*Beat.*

**Mina**    Now!

**Jonno**    Mina . . .

**Mina** *looks to J. Beat. Looks to* **Glory**. *And back to* **Jonno**.

**Mina**    She's right you know.

**Jonno**    What?

**Mina**   Pathetic.

**Jonno**   Don't you start. You heard this Glory?

**Glory**   Me?

*Pause.*

**Jonno**   . . . Take a look in her hand.

*Beat.*

**Jonno**   Go on, what you got there, Glory?

**Glory**   J, I . . . Mina . . .

**Mina**   . . . Show me, I want to see.

*Beat.*

**Glory**   I didn't want . . . You gotta believe, I didn't want . . . I was going to tell you! It's just the once . . . What with him being ill and all I didn't know what I was thinking –

**Mina**   What's in your hand, Glory?

*Beat.* **Glory** *slowly uncurls her fingers . . .*

**Glory**   Just the once . . .

*Beat.*

**Mina**   No. (*Beat.*) Glory . . . (*Beat.*) I knew it all along!

**Glory**   I'm sorry.

**Mina**   Whisperin' Jonno through the letter box like a little whispery rat. You've got a son, Glory! You've got *your* kid!

*Beat.*

**Mina**   Just the once is it?

**Glory**   Yes.

**Mina**   Don't lie to me. Look at the state of you!

**Glory**   I . . .

**Mina**  You fucking have 'n all!

**Glory**  No.

**Mina**  You have!

**Jonno**  Chill, Mina . . .

**Glory**  I'm sorry!

**Mina**  It's ok, it's cool, we can sort this. We just need to think . . . I'll take care of Karli, you do your ickle clucky bit . . . I can pick him up, now. What's the address?

**Glory**  I'm a good mum, Mina.

**Mina**  I'm sorry?

**Glory**  Read to him every night . . . Parks, swimming, all the best clobber, no Primark shit, Min'.

**Mina**  Where is he? I need to go get him, Glory . . .

**Glory**  He's everything to me.

**Mina**  I should think bloody so! For fuck's sake Glory, tell me where he is!

*Beat.*

**Glory**  I asked for help . . . They fucking went and took him Min.

**Mina**  I beg your pardon?

**Glory**  It was getting too much for me –

**Mina**  What?

*Beat.*

**Glory**  I asked for help . . . And they fucking went and took him.

*Beat.*

**Mina**  Who took him?

**Glory**  You know who.

**Mina**   Social services?

**Glory**   They are proper cunts, Min'. I didn't stand a chance.

**Mina**   You, gave him away?

**Glory**   It was Monday morning down fucking Tesco's, you've no idea what it was like, what I was going through.

**Mina**   Really . . .

**Glory**   Those stores are massive. I was lost. Stuck down one aisle after the bastard other. I only wanted eggs. Karli's all nagging on and on at me, 'Mummy . . . can I have this, can I have that?' Blartin', on and on, grabbing things off the shelf. I didn't know what to do, Mina. He wouldn't stop it, he'd been like it for days, clinging and blartin' and nagging, wouldn't leave me alone.

**Mina**   I wonder why that is?

**Glory**   I hadn't slept in weeks and this woman goes to say to me 'Erm . . . S'cuse me love . . . your child . . .' And I want to smash her face in. I want to say to her 'You do it, you look after a screaming, squawking . . . On your own!' I didn't have no one Mina. And in that moment – I want to grab her face and rip it up the shelf but I don't . . . I just . . . stand and . . . panting . . . 'You think I ain't noticed? You think I can't see?' I'm all shouting and screaming and cunting her in my head but I just stand there like a freak, frozen, I can't move my body. She looks at Karlie all with her pity as he grabs a box of eggs, the eggs we've been looking for, and he snatches them off the shelf and I watch him, can't stop him, like in slow motion. He grabs the eggs out the box and starts dropping them on the floor, laughing, and the rage, Mina. I want to kill him. I want to tear him limb from limb. I scare my*self* Min'. He's two years old and I want to stove his head in, I want to grab his head and smash it on the floor like a broken. My own child . . . I said I was sorry! I only ever wanted the best for him. After all those nights of promising . . . I'll never . . . like *her*, fucked up, Special Brew swilling

. . .Then look at me. I don't know what the fuck I'm doing! I see it on tele, all the perfect families, all sat round the tables, laughing, sunshine beaming in, through a kitchen . . . Our gaff? Dippy eggs and coffee? Soldiers to dip in? Taste the difference, Min' . . . I couldn't do it, I *tried*, I can't even *fry* one. I asked for help, I can't be smashing my son's head in!

**Mina**    –

**Glory**    We ain't like them, Min'.

**Mina**    I'm sorry?

**Glory**    Them. Bastards. Yummy mummies.

**Mina**    Since when was it 'we'?

**Glory**    I made sure, I had meetings with them, made sure the foster mum she . . . Is some fat ming but I got her feeding him cabbage.

**Mina**    Oh well then.

**Glory**    I can get him back, soon as I –

**Mina**    Ha.

**Glory**    I was on my own, none, stuck in that rank flat –

**Mina**    Poor you! Poor fucking you!

**Glory**    I tried.

**Mina**    You're his mother, you're supposed to try!

**Glory**    Nothing's ever good enough . . .

**Mina**    My heart bleeds.

**Glory**    You weren't exactly Ma Larkin!

*Beat.*

**Glory**    Mina, I'm sorry.

**Mina**    –

**Jonno**    Mina . . . (*Goes to touch her.*) Sweetheart.

**Mina**   Get the fuck away from me.

**Jonno**   But –

**Mina** (*To* **Jonno**.)   You cunt! How could you!?!

**Jonno**   Me? She begged me.

**Mina**   Serving her up all along is it?

**Jonno**   No . . . And what if I was? It's how we survive!

**Mina**   Survival . . .

**Jonno**   You never complain. I, care, I provide, somebody has to –

**Mina**   And that someone's you is it?

**Jonno**   Yes! Who else is here when the shit hits the fan? She's not, frolickin' off in all her 'Glory'.

**Mina**   The shit hit the fan, Jonno, and you were nowhere to be seen!

**Jonno**   I was right here.

**Mina**   For all the good you –

**Jonno** (*Grabs* **Mina** *and pushes her up against the wall. He holds her there. Beat.*)   Don't say that.

**Mina**   I never wanted money –

**Glory**   Jonno . . .

**Jonno** *and* **Mina** *are up close, eye to eye.*

**Glory**   Jonno, let her go –

**Mina**   You don't even ever look at me, do ya? You never ask how I am.

**Jonno**   I tried –

**Mina**   Tried so hard you're serving up?

**Jonno**   Saving up to get you away from –

**Mina**   You never even asked me if I wanted to go Jonno!

**Jonno**   I can't get a word in. You don't stop rabbiting on about shit and with your relentless scrubbing –

**Mina**   I don't want to go to Scotland! I never did, not with –

**Jonno**   Don't . . .

**Mina**   My warrior . . . My William Wallace, look at cha. So heroic . . . Between us . . . nothing . . . it's like, a hole, an echo, we ain't even touched since –

**Jonno** *grabs* **Mina**'s *neck.*

**Mina**   Go on. Go on, fuck me up, I dare you.

*Beat.*

**Mina**   You can't even get it up.

**Jonno** *gets more angry, like he can't contain it any more.*

**Mina** *is choking.*

**Jonno** *squeezes her hard against the cupboards on the wall . . .*

**Glory**   Jonno, stop it. Jonno. You're hurting her!

**Glory** *tries to pull him off.* **Jonno** *carries on squeezing, oblivious to* **Glory**. **Mina** *and* **Jonno** *look each other straight in the eye.*

**Glory**   Jonno.

**Mina**   Pussy. (*Coughing and spluttering.*) Think you could ever hurt me more than it already hurts in –

**Jonno** *punches past* **Mina**'s *head to the cupboard. He punches it hard. He punches it again and again. Putting his fist right through.*

**Jonno**   Raaa! Fucking fuck! (*He keeps punching and pounding. He stops.*)

*Beat.*

**Jonno** *staggers back, letting* **Mina** *go. Beat. He slowly sinks to the floor. He bows his head.*

**Jonno**  Fuck.

*Silence.*

**Mina** *sinks to the floor next to him.*

**Jonno** (*With his head in his hands.*)  I'm sorry, Min'.

*Beat.*

**Mina**  It's ok.

**Jonno**  I never wanted any of this.

**Mina**  I know . . .

**Jonno**  I never meant to hurt you.

**Mina**  Yes, I know.

**Jonno**  How . . .?

**Mina**  Shh . . .

**Jonno**  I don't know . . .

**Mina**  Shh . . . My love . . . My warrior.

*She strokes his head. She looks at his fist and kisses it. She holds him. They hold each other on the floor.*

**Jonno**  She was . . .

**Mina** *pecks his head with a gentle kiss.*

**Jonno** (*He looks at her.*)  I fucking love you, Mina.

**Mina**  I know. I know you do.

*She holds him.*

*Beat.*

**Jonno**  I miss her.

*They rock slightly hugging each other on the floor.*

*Beat.*

**Glory**  You for real?

*Beat.*

**Glory**   Seriously . . . forgive him? Just like that?

**Mina** (**Mina** *turns to look at* **Glory**.)   And what if I am?

**Glory**   If it wasn't f' him I wouldn't be in this mess!

**Mina**   Make you take it did he?

**Glory**   No but . . . he was well up for it!

**Mina**   Have you heard yourself? (*She goes to get up to look at* **Glory**, *leaving* **Jonno** *on the floor.*)

**Glory**   It wasn't my fault, I asked for help.

*Beat.*

**Mina**   You had it all, Glory . . . beautiful, great tits, poetry. They wet me up you know, the gals on the wing, boiling hot sugar. Look! (*Shows scar on her neck.*) It sticks. But so long as you're alright, hunky-dory-Glory, swanning off, leaving me, here, stuck, scuttling about like a shit, a scuttly little . . . Desperate . . . But it's never enough, Glory, it would never be enough to bring her –

*Beat.*

**Glory**   You were a good mum.

**Jonno**   Things happen –

**Mina**   Ok.

**Glory**   You couldn't put her down for six months. Like a barnacle she was, stuck t' y' –

**Mina**   We were animals. This place was like Naga-fucking-saki.

**Glory**   We did the best we –

**Mina**   Really?

**Glory**   We did what we had to.

**Mina**    Fucking joke! Our 'Brave little warrior' Maia. That's
what her name means. She had asthma, couldn't breathe.
She'd have to be made of raw iron bolts to put up with the
likes of us innit? (*Beat.*) I remember that night and no matter
how hard I try no to . . . Stood in her bedroom –

**Glory**    Mina you don't have to –

**Mina**    I was just trying to settle her. Her chest going up and
down crazy, She kept dropping her bottle and sucking at
nothing, she'd not been like this for months and I decide,
then and there, Glory, Im not going out, I'm not leaving. I
don't give a mother fucking flying winky if its my bastard
turn, and she and I and we and eyes like butterfly (*Beat.*)
And then I hear you, scraping for crack crumbs, Glory,
through the little gap in the door, sat on your hands and
knees scraping your martel pipe, like an insect. And do you
know what you say to me?

**Glory** (*Beat*) No.

**Mina**    Hum?

**Glory**    No.

**Mina**    You don't say nothing. Sweet fucking sod all. You
don't have to. You just look at me with your desperate,
gaping, pleading eyes.

**Glory**    Those punters the night before, they were rough,
Min'.

**Mina**    Diddums.

**Glory**    I was like bleeding.

**Mina**    Pathetic.

**Glory**    We were all bang in trouble, clucking our tits off –

**Mina**    I didn't care about getting sick.

**Glory**    Yes you did! He did anyway! (*To* **Jonno**.) And where
the hell were you?

**Jonno**  Grafting. I told you, there was Feds round every corner –

**Glory**  Ha!

**Jonno**  It was on-top.

**Mina** (*To* **Glory**.)  You're the one we agreed would stay! You're the one that looked at me . . . you promised –

**Glory**  You were gone for hours.

**Mina**  You know what it's like for me and there was loads of 'em out that evening, little, skanky, skinny, white things, sexy, and I couldn't find a spot and then when I do first bloke, a fiver! And that takes 45 minutes! So I have to do another *and* another, *and* . . . I have to keep going, gotta make enough for Glory, all the while thinking . . . trying not to think, not thinking –

**Glory**  Mina . . .

**Mina**  And then . . . (*Beat.*) I'm about to get in this knob-jocks Volvo, Nigey-fuck and he's all 'Hey, mama . . . I love fat gally,' and when he says twenty quid I'm thinking cel-eb-ration and I'm just about to get in his car when . . . suddenly (*Beat.*) I can't breathe . . . it's like it's got me, round my neck and got in here (*Taps heart.*) and it's . . . I know something's up. In my gut it's got me. I slam the car door shut and he looks so pissed off, he offers me more money but now I'm off and –

**Glory**  Mina –

**Mina**  Running . . . Fast as I can as the sun is struggling –

**Glory**  I'm sorry. I'm fucking sorry, ok?

**Mina**  But when I get to the house you know what I see?

**Jonno**  You don't have to do this.

**Mina**  Do ya? Do you know what I see? (*Beat.*) Blue lights, an ambulance flashing and I think it must be the old feller at number 43, so I run up the stairs, sort of hoping, praying it's not you or J, but when I get to the door, *our* door, and I get out my key the door just swings open and . . . J sat on the sofa, eyes fixed, he looks up to me and . . . and before I know it –

**Jonno**   I don't know what to say.

**Mina**   You grab –

**Jonno**   You start screaming

**Mina**   Holding me back.

**Jonno**   I won't let you in. You are clawing –

**Mina**   I want to see. I want to fucking see . . . (*Beat.*) And then these two ambulance kookies step out of her room like they own the place and they start talking. One of them on and on jibberish. I watch her lips. Her nasty little cracked lips and soon . . . She's been smoking! Ambulance fucking dashy smoking and her nasty little arse ring mouth . . .

**Jonno**   You don't move.

**Mina**   Starts sucking. Sucking it all up, all the life and colour and –

**Jonno**   I don't know what the fuck I'm supposed to do!

**Mina**   And leaving me with nothing. Just grey. Day after day, never ending . . . 45 minutes to die . . . Collapsed lung. That's what they said apparently. If we had found her . . . Got there sooner. Asthma see . . . (*Beat.*) Like ice when they found her, Glory, and you'd just popped out –

**Glory**   I was only gone for ten minutes.

**Mina**   Ten minutes?

**Glory**   I thought . . . I was yacking up ma ring, no good to anyone. I couldn't . . . I thought t' . . . he's only down the back alley, ten minutes, five tops, sort me out . . . I tried to call you, left messages repeatedly –

**Mina**   I was busy!

**Glory**    It broke my heart too, you know!

*Beat.*

**Mina**    Yeah?

**Glory**    'Course it fucking did.

**Mina**    You have no idea.

**Glory**    Min' –

**Mina**    When they took her that night –

**Glory**    I came back.

**Mina**    You rock up all eyes glazing –

**Glory**    I didn't know . . . We were all in shock, Min'.

**Mina**    Police coming any minute . . . And I'm all set, ready to tell them you . . . You did it. You fucking . . .! I grab your hair –

**Glory**    Hurting –

**Mina**    Pin you down, I'm not letting you fucking go till they get you. I could gouge your eyes out, digging my nails in . . . and then you tell me you're pregnant. (*Beat.*) Out it pops. You tell me you're pregnant . . . with Karli.

**Glory**    I am. I was.

**Mina**    And in that moment I know that you have got to get away, that he, Karli, is the most important thing, that good must come of this. And so I . . . So I . . . Do you want to see what's in the fucking boxes, Glory? Do you wanna fucking see?

**Jonno**    Mina don't –

**Mina**    I'll show you. I'll bloody show you what's in the boxes. (**Mina** *starts emptying the cardboard boxes. She pulls out old kids' toys and clothes and holds it up to show* **Glory**.) Look, toys, I want you to look, Glory . . . Look in the boxes! Tigger, look, and bastard Pooh! Saved, all for you . . . Boxed up, neat, no sign of little fucking Piglet through . . . Where is the fuck is the shit? Cunt done a runner, eh? (*Throws teds to the floor, churning out more stuff . . .*) The Faraway Tree . . . sack of shit that is . . .. (*She throws copy of Famous Five at the wall. She points at the Early Years' book.*) The Twits, The Early Years What To Expect, the unex-fucking-pected eh, Glory? (*Continues emptying boxes.*) Hamsters . . . chickens . . . And what the . . .? (*Holds up unidentifiable soft ted. A small mechanical dog sat in front of her does a little involuntary somersault. She picks it up and throws it at the wall.*) Agh, Shit!!! (*Beat. Turns to* **Glory**.) You have no idea.

**Glory**   I never knew –

**Mina**   No.

*Beat.*

**Glory**   I –

**Mina**   When I went to her bedroom . . . after they'd . . . When she'd . . . They'd bailed me, two weeks and I thought I best go clear it, sort it all out for J or something. I thought I'll just bolt in, get it over with but when I get in . . . When I stand by the door, when I see her cot and . . . clothes strewn, still smelling . . . covers ruffled and the whole of it . . . The whole of it like . . . Even the giraffes on the mobile thing hang . . . and I like them not moving, we hold our breath.

**Mina** *suddenly runs down the hall and stands to the door of her daughter's bedroom.*

**Mina**   Fuck! Fucking . . . ! (*She kicks the door through with one big boot of her foot.*)

*Pause. She stands at the entrance to the broken door . . . she inhales. Beat. She goes into the room.*

**Glory** (*To* **Jonno**.)   She gonna be alright?

**Jonno**   Fuck up.

**Glory**   She ain't taking it well.

**Jonno**  D' ya think?

*Silence.*

*After some time* **Mina** *emerges slowly.*

**Mina**  In handcuffs I was at the funeral . . . Screws stood either side of me, photographers sneaking, hiding in bushes, like little fucking snipers. No family, no . . . And J, head buried deep in his coat, won't even give me eyes and I can't cry. I can't cry, Glory. I can't have no rant, no scream, no breakdown in Tesco for me. They called me evil, in the papers, evil! Front page! And so I have to stand, cold, stone faced, frantically gulping. I've got this bunch of petals in my pocket, I took 'em off this bunch of flowers the coppers got me, red, like claret. And I want to chuck 'em, I want to sprinkle them onto her coffin, that's all I'm wanting but I can't even do that . . . There's this thing inside and it's like its ripping, rips a fucking hole in space and time and won't stop ripping and so I keep the petals scrunched up in my pockets till I don't know if it's them or me that's claret. Bleeding.

*Beat.*

**Jonno**  It wasn't your fault.

**Mina**  No?

**Jonno**  Mina . . .

**Mina**  Wasn't it?

**Jonno**  No, sweetheart –

**Mina**  I think it was.

*Beat.*

**Mina**  Her lungs collapsed and no one noticed. Traces of crack, J.

*Beat.*

**Glory**  Mina . . . I'm so sorry. (*Beat.*) Truly, deeply –

**Mina**    Get that out of my house. (*Gestures gear on the table.*)

**Jonno**    What?

**Mina**    I mean it.

**Jonno**    But . . .

**Mina**    Fucking get rid. I don't care what or how or who or whatever, just fucking get rid of it!

*Beat.*

**Mina** *jumps up and shoves the drugs and paraphernalia into* **Jonno**'*s hands.*

*Beat.*

**Jonno**    Ok. (*Touches* **Mina**'*s hand.*)

**Mina** (*Looks at* **Jonno** . . .)

**Jonno**    Ok, I will.

**Mina**    And get some bloody milk while you're at it. There's change in my purse and . . . Get sommat for breaky.

**Jonno** *rattles his pocket to show he's got change.*

**Mina**    Thank you.

**Jonno** *goes to leave.*

**Mina** (*She shouts after him.*)    And stick a bloody coat on, you'll catch your death out, it's freezing.

*He turns and smiles at her. He grabs his coat. He looks at her, puts it on.*

**Mina**    Bloody buffoon . . .

*He leaves.*

*Pause.*

**Glory**    Fuckin' hell, Mina.

**Mina** *goes to get up.*

**Glory**    Shit.

*Beat.*

**Glory**    You alright?

**Mina** *turns to look at* **Glory**.

**Glory**    What's it all about, Min'?

*Beat.*

**Glory** (*Laughs nervously.*)    Innit?

*Pause.*

**Glory**    They are such cunts, Mina. Seriously, I tried my best, they don't fucking listen. I asked for, like, parenting course or something and –

**Mina**    You won't change will you?

**Glory**    What? I am . . . I will . . .

**Mina**    You can't keep running for ever, Glory.

**Glory**    I'm not.

**Mina**    What happened?

**Glory**    I'm gonna get him back, it's not for ever.

**Mina**    I mean, to us?

*Beat.*

**Glory**    I can get clean. I could even stop here and –

**Mina**    Show me.

**Glory**    What?

**Mina**    Your hand. Open it. Let me see.

**Glory**    Min', really. I'll go to doctors, we could go now, you could come with me.

**Mina**    Show me.

**Glory** *hesitates.*

**Mina** –

**Glory** *uncurls her fingers.*

*Beat.*

**Mina** Ok . . .

*Beat.*

**Mina** *turns away.*

**Glory** I'm just gonna sort myself out then I'm good to go, chat scripts anything –

**Mina** Do you know why I smashed that girl's head in?

**Glory** What?

**Mina** The girl who picked on Catherine wheel. Why I smashed her head in?

*Beat.*

**Glory** No.

**Mina** Because I couldn't handle it. I couldn't handle the guilt of it.

*Pause.*

**Glory** I know. I know what you're saying . . .

**Mina** Do ya?

**Glory** Yes, 'course I –

*Beat.*

**Glory** Really . . . I'm scared, Min'.

**Mina** Scared.

**Glory** I'm bloody petrified . . . Out there. On my own. Without . . .

*Beat.*

**Glory**  I can't cope. I need you.

**Mina**  You don't need me.

**Glory**  I've got no one. Mina please –

**Mina**  I'm not your fucking mum!

*Beat.*

**Mina**  You hear me?

**Glory**  I know that. You think I don't know that?

**Mina**  I can't help you.

**Glory**  Mina . . .

**Mina**  For fuck's sake.

**Glory**  It's cold out.

**Mina**  Just go.

**Glory**  But it's freezing. I go, sort myself, stop just a couple of –

**Mina**  Please.

**Glory**  Is this really what you want?

**Mina**  Yes. It is.

**Glory** *puts the drugs in her pocket.*

**Mina**  It is.

**Glory** (*Gets up. She grabs her coat and bag.*)   Ok, ok, I will, but I'm gonna get help you know.

**Mina**  Good.

**Glory**  Seriously,

**Mina**  I hope so.

*They look at each other. Beat.*

**Mina**  Take care.

*Beat.*

**Glory**  I want to do this, Mina.

**Mina**  I know. (*Beat.*) My coat. Take it. (*She reaches for her coat and gives it to* **Glory**.)

**Glory**  Thanks.

**Mina**  And the jumper. Keep it.

**Glory** (*Slightly sarcastic.*)  Thank you.

**Mina**  Bobble hat? Beret?

**Glory**  Yer daft-head, you.

*They look at each other and laugh slightly. Nervous. Beat.*

**Mina**  Giz a bloody hug then.

**Glory**  Mina, I love you.

*They hug. For a long time.*

**Glory**  I am gonna get him back. If it's the last thing I do.

**Mina** *breaks their embrace.*

**Mina**  I know you will.

**Glory**  And I'll bring him round, to visit.

**Mina**  That would be lovely.

**Glory**  Promise.

**Mina**  Look after yourself, Glory.

*Beat.*

**Glory**  Ok.

*Exit* **Glory**.

**Mina** *goes to put the kettle on. She gets an old mug out . . . hesitates, changes her mind. She comes back into the living room. She looks at the posh tea set, the untouched spotty mugs and teapot, she smiles slightly. She picks up one of the nice cups, one of the ones saved for* *special occasions. She turns it over, in her hand. She lays out one of the nice spotty mugs and the teapot, ready for her to use. She pauses. The TV catches her eye . . . The kettle flicks to the boil. She goes to the kitchen. She returns with tea bags milk and kettle. She pours water into the teapot and puts it neatly on the table. She puts the kettle back in the kitchen, she comes back into the living room. She pours her tea out of the teapot into her special cup, she adds milk. She picks up her mug of tea and goes to the balcony. She opens the curtains wide and the door. She goes out onto the balcony. She looks up to the sky, the horizon, and breathes in fresh air. She looks up to the sky, she blows on her cup of tea, huddling for warmth. She lowers her cup of tea and breathes.*

*'On the Nature of Daylight' by Max Richter plays as the lights fade.*

Along my life's unusual and very erratic journey I have encountered many larger-than-life characters, a significant proportion of them miscreants. *The Monkey,* my first play, features four characters and in them I have attempted to capture the many traits of a London sub-culture of addiction and criminality that most people never come into contact with. Dark comedy has always appealed to me and in that vein I wrote *The Monkey* which highlights the problems that can arise when you don't pay your debts.

John Stanley

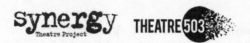

Synergy Theatre Project in association with Theatre503

# The Monkey

## By John Stanley

*The Monkey* was first performed at Theatre503
on 7 March 2017.

## Cast

| | |
|---|---|
| **Terry (known as Tel)** | Morgan Watkins |
| **Darren (known as Dal)** | Daniel Kendrick |
| **Rebecca (known as Becks)** | Danielle Flett |
| **Alan (known as Thick-Al)** | George Whitehead |

| | |
|---|---|
| *Director* | Russell Bolam |
| *Designer* | Katy McPhee |
| *Costume Designer* | Emmett de Monterey |
| *Lighting Designer* | Rob Youngson |
| *Sound Designer* | Rebecca Smith |
| *Casting Director* | Nadine Rennie CDG |
| *Production Manager* | Steve Wald |
| *Stage Manager* | Rike Berg |
| *Assistant Stage Manager* | Karl Smith |
| *Assistant* | Carrie Rock |
| *Fight Director* | Malcolm Ranson |
| *Dialect Coach* | Hazel Holder |

Please note that the text of the play which appears in this volume may be changed during the rehearsal process and appear in a slightly altered form in performance.

Supported by

 CALOUSTE GULBENKIAN
FOUNDATION
UK BRANCH

# John Stanley

# The Monkey

**Rebecca**, **Alan** *and* **Darren** *live in a drab, 8-storey council tower block in Bermondsey, in the borough of Southwark, London.* **Terry** *used to live nearby, in Bermondsey, but now he lives in neighbouring Deptford. All four have heroin habits and all make their money from various forms of criminality.*

*The first act is next to the lift and moves to the stairs. Everything else takes place in the lounge of* **Alan**'s *flat.*

*Description of lounge: As people enter into* **Alan**'s *flat they are in a small passage area. A few jackets are hanging on the wall and a door opposite leads to the bedroom. The lounge is painted in a faded beige colour, blue carpet squares on the floor, a small kitchenette in an adjoining area. A well-worn, dark red, two-seat settee rests against the wall and a matching armchair is at the side of the settee. In front of the settee is a white melamine table. In the middle of the opposite wall there is a large window and next to it a unit housing a stereo system with a television on the top. Sitting on the television is a clock. Two speakers are positioned at either end of the wall. Cables hang from the speakers to the stereo. To the left (as you enter the lounge from the passageway) two high-back chairs are positioned against the wall and next to them is a shelving unit with a cupboard at the bottom. Next to the shelving unit is a pedal bin.*

**Terry** *(known as Tel) is 32 years old. With short brown hair styled with a side parting, he is 6' 4", good-looking, muscular and confident. He always wears a suit with a shirt and tie and takes pride in his appearance.*

**Darren** *(known as Dal) is 32 years old. He is 5' 9", with fair hair, boyish looks and a slim build. Scruffy when he's not working, he is easy-going and could easily be taken for a 25-year-old.*

**Rebecca** *(known as Becks) is 31 years old. 5' 6" with long fair hair, she is petite and outspoken and as well as looking younger than she is you wouldn't make her out as a drug addict.*

**Alan** *(known as thick-Al), 5' 8" and 21 years old, has dark, long hair and is overweight and a little dim.*

## Act One

*Monday morning just after eleven, a tower block in Bermondsey. On the ground floor waiting for the lift to arrive is* **Terry**.

**Darren** *and* **Rebecca** *walk out of the staircase recess. Deep in conversation they don't notice* **Terry** *(who is slightly obscured by the lift-shaft wall) and carry on past.*

**Terry**  Oy, oyyy . . . Dal, Becks.

*Taken by surprise,* **Darren** *and* **Rebecca** *stop and turn their heads.*

**Darren**  Oh fuck, Tel. Ya gimme a right fright. Ain't seen ya in ages mate. Good t' see ya.

**Rebecca**  Yeah, bin a long time, gotta be well over a year now since I see ya.

**Terry**  Yeah well, bin busy in I?

**Rebecca** *and* **Darren** *move closer towards* **Terry** *and they remain talking in the same position.*

**Rebecca**  Still like a whistle, eh?

**Terry**  Course, that'll never change. Always wear a whistle me, shirt an tie. An me daisies'r always polished. (**Terry** *lifts his boot and points at it.*) Um a smart guy.

**Rebecca**  Yeah ya are. 'Ere Tel, there's somefink diffrent boutcha. Yuv done somefink.

**Terry**  It's me railins init?

**Terry** *gives a forced smile and points to his teeth.*

**Rebecca**  Oh yeah, yeah. They look the biz.

**Terry**  Fer twenty large mate, they oughta.

**Darren**  Gawd, that's some dosh. But them railins look great now mate. Ere, ope ya dun mind me askin like, but ya managin t' keep on toppa fings. Ya know like, ya oldin it down ok these days, Tel?

**Terry**   Wotcha talkin bout, Dal?

**Darren**   Oh c'mon, Tel, ya know, ya know what um sayin.

**Terry**   No I dunno wotcha sayin. Ya oldin it down ok these days are ya?

**Darren**   C'mon, Tel, ya know what I mean. We're yer mates. Jus wanna know yer ok. That's all.

**Terry**   Yeah well, course um ok. Oldin it down jus fine in I? Oldin it down good, alright?

**Darren**   Yeah alright Tel, that's great. Good t' ear it, mate.

**Terry**   S' dun tell me ya two are an item now?

**Rebecca**   No way. We might work t'gever but that's it. Jus the forta me an im bein an item. Ya gotta be kiddin. Ud sooner lose a leg.

**Darren** (*To* **Rebecca**.)   Bout sooner lose a leg. Yud love the chance, Becks.

**Rebecca**   Yeah, in what world's that? Ya drop ints by the fousand an I aint never acted on one yet ave I?

**Darren**   Ya got sum mouf on yer, ya ave girl. (*To* **Terry**.) She's still gotta big mouf ain't she, Tel?

**Terry**   She as. Wooden be the same Becks if she weren't moufy.

**Darren**   Yeah, spose. Wotcha doin wiv yerself, Tel? Ya aint still out drummin are ya?

**Terry**   Nah I aint, not really. Though if someone clues me up bout a drum then I might fink bout doin it. Bin doin plenty a ugly an that gets me froo.

**Darren**   What's ugly?

**Terry**   Ugly pratt, this n that. This n that init mate?

**Darren**  Oh right.

**Rebecca**  I aint never earda that one before, Tel.

**Darren**  Nah, me neever.

**Terry**  Nah, it's one a mine init.

**Darren**  Good one mate. S' ya makin a few quid or what doin ugly?

**Terry**  Um makin plent-ee doin ugly, fanks. An ugly right now is dealin in moody gear. Fake clobber, iPhone screens, fags, ya name it I gotit. Makin a right killin I am.

**Darren**  Twenty large on railins ya gotta be.

**Terry**  Tellin ya mate I am.

**Rebecca**  Let us in on the secret Tel?

**Terry**  Got meself away frum the grasses an losers round ere, didn't I? Plotted up in me uncle's ol drum in Deptford I keep me ead down. An I keep me wits about me. Look about, see what's goin on. An I take advantage when I can wiv whatever I can. An I never let no cunts ave me over. (*Pause.*) What bout yous two? Still workin airports an stations?

**Darren**  Shows ow long ya aint seen us, Tel. Can't remember last time we worked an airport or station. Airports an stations'r bad news. Aint they, Becks?

**Rebecca**  Dal, ow wood I know bout workin an airport? I ain't never worked an airport. Not on me own an not wiv you. An I only worked a station wiv ya once. We never got a bean.

**Darren**  Ya aint never worked an airport wiv me? That's strange, me memory's well fucked. Mus be all them drugs. Anyway, dun matter where ya go these days it's camera'd up, init Tel? Airports an stations are da worse. But there's still rich pickins in uvver places. Where tourists ang round, that's where we ang out. Always a camera somewhere that's gonna get ya though. Curse a fieves they are mate, them cameras.

So ya gotta be shrewd. I got sum right good gear off ebay.
Wigs, beards, moustaches, ya name it. Got a selection a ats.
All sorts a different cloves. Smart, caj. Look different all the
time when I go out. T' be onest, Tel, when um done up an
um sittin there in fronta the mirra I can't recognise meself,
look like a right cunt I do. But it's gotta be done or ya get
nicked fer sure.

**Rebecca** (*To* **Darren**.)   I ain't never told ya this but I fink ya
look much better, almost alf decent *wiv* the disguises.

**Darren**   Oh, very amusin. Ilarious. Ere, Becks, tell im what
*you* wear t' go out.

**Rebecca**   Why d' I need t' tell im that?

**Darren**   Go on tell im. Tel'll like it when e ears.

**Rebecca**   Fuck off Dal, alright. Yer a right mixer, ya are.
Shut yer mouf.

**Terry**   Ere, ere fer fuck's sake. Ud never do no work wiv
yous. Yud right get on me nerves bick-rin all day.

**Rebecca**   There ain't no bick-rin. E does what I tell im
when we're workin. I got the ideas an e aint.

**Darren**   Oh yeah, brilliant, Becks. She finks the fings up an
I do em. That's er. Ere, Tel, ull tell ya what she won't tell ya.
She gets dressed up in skirts an igh eels. Uses different wigs.
An wiv er make-up ya wooden recognise er. Normal times ya
only ever see er in trackies but when she's out workin, she
looks tasty, a right sort.

**Rebecca**   Ya dun need disguises t' make ya look like a cunt,
Dal. Ya already are one.

**Terry**   Kids, kids. Ere, Becks, I ain't never seen ya in a skirt
let alone igh eels. I betcha look the biz.

**Rebecca**   I look classy, Tel. Diffrent t' what I look like in
me trackies.

**Terry**   I see ya got a 'Juicy' on.

**Terry** *looks closely at the 'Juicy' tracksuit that* **Rebecca** *is wearing.*

**Terry**    Can tell it's a moody. But as it goes it's a goodun. Pound t' a pincha shit it's one a mine. All me moodies are da biz. Next time um about ull bring ya down a selection.

**Rebecca**    Ok. Ud preciate that. Size small.

**Terry**    Done. Ya know Becks, I always forta lotta ya. Ya know that. Sorta fort one day ya an me coulda bin an item.

**Rebecca**    Tel, we're mates. An we aint suited t' be an item.

**Terry**    Dunno why not?

**Rebecca**    Well one big problem, Tel, is I dun fancy ya.

**Terry**    Me motto's never say never.

*Beat.*

**Terry**    Ya earnin a few bob the two a yers or what?

**Rebecca**    Yeah we're earnin regular. We split the money down the middle an we do ok. But I wanna stop all the feevin, get off the gear an go t' college. Get a proper job. I bin ere all me life an I jus wanna get the fuck away, outa Bermondsey. Go an live somewhere nice. Maybe down the coast. Bournemuff, somewhere like that.

**Darren**    Listen t' er bollocks. Wants t' live in fuckin Bournemuff. She aint never even bin there. Always sayin the same ol shit. Ere Tel, she's jus come outa re-ab, again. Was only six monfs ago she was in re-ab the last time. Was there fer two fuckin monfs an now anuvver two monfs. An I gotta work on me own every time she finks she can clean up. She come out two weeks ago an jus bout lasted a week. Straight back on the gear.

**Rebecca**    Oh shut up. If ya was me proper mate yud try t' show me sum encouragement.

**Darren**    I do.

**Rebecca**   Oh yeah, when? Um goin now. Off t' me mum's, probly stay over s' dun come lookin fer me Dal. See ya, Tel. Laters, Dal.

**Darren**   Yeah laters Becks.

**Terry**   Yeah, see ya soon Becks. Nice t' see ya girl.

**Rebecca** *exits*.

**Darren**   Fink I'll be off too, mate . . .

**Terry**   Ang on Dal, we'll ave a chat. Come on, sit on the stairs fer a few minutes wiv me.

**Darren**   Oh . . . oh, ok Tel.

**Terry** *takes a packet of tissues from his pocket, removes one and wipes the part of the step where he's about to sit. He looks at the step closely, takes another tissue from his pocket, wipes the step some more and takes a plastic bag from his other pocket and puts the used tissues in it. He puts the plastic bag back in his pocket and then he sits down.* **Darren** *sits next to him and takes out a packet of cigarettes.*

**Terry**   Wotcha doin?

**Darren**   Avin a fag.

**Terry**   Not round me mate, ya know I dun smoke.

**Darren**   Oh yeah, yeah, right, Tel.

**Darren** *puts the packet of cigarettes back in his pocket.*

**Terry**   Ere, Becks dun change. Always says what she finks, dun she?

**Darren**   Yep, always will. But it's true she aint elpin erself bein round users all the time.

**Terry**   She aint. But fing is t' clean up ya jus gotta get the willpower t'gever.

**Darren**   Yeah, mate. That's right. Uv tried dozens a times t' clean up but I reckon I got me abit fer life.

**Terry**   Ya might ave but not me mate. No way. I definitely
aint got me abit fer life. When I see olduns still on the gear I
fink t' meself I aint *never* gonna end up like them.

**Darren**   I ope not, Tel. We done well when we went out
drummin t'gever, didn't we, mate? An we ad a right laugh.
Fuck, those was good times mate.

**Terry**   Yeah those was. Good times. Seems like a long time
go now though, lot's appened. But we always ad a right good
laugh. Stopped when I got done though dinit?

**Darren**   Yeah, but the main fing is yer ok now. Yer better.
That's the main fing.

**Terry**   Yeah that is the main fing. I old me temper better an
I never ear them voices no more. Get an occasional lousy
now an again but that's it.

**Darren**   What the fuck's a lousy, Tel?

**Terry**   Lousy lisper init mate, whisper. Lousy lisper, whisper.

**Darren**   Oh right, right. But I aint never earda lousy lisper.
What the fuck's a lousy lisper?

**Terry**   It's someone ooh can't speak proper init? Someone
ooh fuckin lisps.

**Darren**   Oh right, yeah. Gotit. Meself, I dunno no one ooh
lisps. Must be a cunt that t' lisp. Anyway Tel, wiv the voices
gone, part frum the occasional lousy that is, an ya oldin yer
temper better. It's all good news mate. Ya jus gotta stay calm
Tel. An dun let fings get t'cha.

**Terry**   I do stay calm an I dun let fings get t' me no more,
Dal. I sort em out mate. Ere, Dal, I know I told ya before, but
ya know ull always be grateful don'tcha? Always be grateful ya
never fucked off an left me. I wooden be ere now mate. Not
many wooder phoned fer elp an stayed. Not many wooder
done that, Dal. Ull never forget it. Never forget it mate.

**Darren**   I know yer grateful, Tel. I know that.

**Terry**   Angin round waitin fer the ambulance. Fuck me, mate, coulda meant ya takin a term.

**Darren**   Coulda but I never s' it dun matter. Um jus pleased ya got better Tel.

**Terry**   Yeah. But ya know what, Dal? There's times, certain times when I fink back. Like now while we're talkin. Um finkin back t' that fuckin drum.

**Darren**   Dun fink back, Tel. That's the best fing mate. Jus dun fink back. There's no need.

**Terry**   What, dya fink I do it on purpose or somefink? (*Then raising his voice.*) That what ya fink?

**Darren**   No I dun fink that, Tel. I was jus like sayin, that's all like. Fink back as much as ya want mate.

**Terry**   Yeah well, ok. I dunno why I went up that poxy ladder in the first fuckin place. Never made no sense, still dun. I never done a drum usin a ladder before. Always went froo the front door, sometimes the back door. I ain't never smashed a winda t' get inta a drum. Ya ever smashed a winda t' get inta a drum, Dal?

**Darren**   I aint really a drummer am I, Tel? But when I was out wiv ya ya always went froo a door.

**Terry**   'Course I did. Cut yerself easy on windas. It's unprofessional an ya can leave evidence. Dya remember the doors a that drum, Dal?

**Darren**   Oh yeah, Tel, ull always remember the doors a *that* drum. Ull never forget em. Neever a the fuckers'd budge. Couldn't force a gap wide nuff t' get the fuckin crow in.

**Terry**   That's right, mate. Ya jus dunno ow often uv fort bout them fuckin doors. Outa the blue I can jus suddenly start finkin bout them doors. Fort about em an fort about em. But now I understand. Them lousies clued me up. An fanks t' them I know why we couldn't get froo them fuckin doors. Ya know what they was made frum, don'tcha Dal?

**Darren**  No, Tel, what was they made frum?

**Terry**  They was made frum Kryptonite, mate. That's what they was made frum.

**Darren**  Kryptonite, Tel!!?

**Terry**  Yeah, mazin eh?

**Darren**  But Tel there ain't no Kryptonite. Them lousies got it wrong, mate. Kryptonite's frum *Superman* comics. Superman's frum the planet Krypton. An when the planet blows up the bits a Krypton that're left fall t' earf. An if ever Superman comes across a bita Kryptonite . . .

**Terry** (*Interrupting and raising his voice.*)  Dun matter, it dun matter. What appened wiv Superman, Dal, dun matter. Fing is, everyfink in them comics is modelled on real life. An that ouse wiv them doors musta belonged t' sum massive wealfy geez. An e ad access t' sum Kryptonite. An e made the fuckin doors frum it. Alright!?

**Darren**  Okay, Tel, yeah ok mate. Good ya sussed that out. Well done. Lucky fer Superman e never tried t' get inta *that* drum.

**Terry**  Why's that?

**Darren**  Oh it dun matter Tel. Anyway, bofe them doors were right fuckers, that's all I know. Cunt of a drum that was.

**Terry**  Fuckin was. But a result the ladder was in the fuckin shed though weren't it?

**Darren**  Wotcha talkin bout, Tel? Considerin what appened, I wooden say it was a result.

**Terry** (*With raised voice.*)  Now come on. It was a result findin the fuckin ladder at the time we found it. Um re-tellin the fuckin story an the part um at is before I fell off the fuckin ladder. Right?

**Darren**   Yeah, yeah ok Tel. Stay calm mate. I know yer re-tellin the story but I was there, dun forget, an I already know the story.

**Terry** (*Raising his voice more and speaking in a menacing manner.*) I know ya know the fuckin story, Dal. Dun mean ya can't spend a cupla minutes listenin t' me re-tellin the fuckin story. It obviously weren't no result when I look back on it. Fallin off the fucker an landin on me ead gimme times when I aint got no control. Never used t' be like that.

**Darren**   Yeah, Tel, ya never. I know. Now ya jus gotta old it down. Uv seen ya nuff times when ya lose control an it ain't pleasant. Nearly shit meself when ya ad a go at Micky.

**Terry**   Shut it bout that, right!

**Darren**   Yeah, yeah, Tel, sorry mate. (*Beat.*) Ya aint ere t' see fick-Al are ya?

**Terry**   I am as it goes. Come t' ave a cuppa wiv im. Ain't bin up ere in awhile. If I adn't bumped inta ya an Becks ud ave popped in t' see yers as well. Now um doin mosta me biz in Deptford, Bermondsey's a bit out me way.

**Darren**   Spose. Ya know fick-Al's got some ace brown. Shit deals but worf it cos a the strengf a the gear.

**Terry**   What am I earin!? Ya tellin me fick-Al's started dealin again?

**Darren**   Well it ain't dealin proper like. Ere, dun say I said nuffink will ya? E's jus sellin t' the few of us users in the block like. Ya know, ya know like. Jus between us lot ere like. I fort that was why ya was ere, Tel. T' get sum gear off im.

**Terry**   As it goes it weren't. An wadya mean between us lot ere?

**Darren**   Ya know what I mean, Tel. There's me an Dean on the fird. Jack an Sam below us on the second. Becks on the fiff. Ang on, is that it, aint there no one else? Me an Dean, Jack an Sam . . . Becks, oh yeah, course, yeah there's fick-Al on the sixf. Ow many's that?

**Terry**    Six in total, Dal.

**Darren**    Right, yeah six of us. Yeah, that's right.

*At this point a man, about 40 years old, walks towards the stairs and tries to force a gap between* **Terry** *and* **Darren** *so he can walk up.* **Terry** *grabs his leg and pushes him back.*

**Terry**    Oy ya cunt. Ooh ya fuckin pushin past?

**Man**    I'm just trying to get up the stairs to my flat. I live here.

**Terry**    Well aintcha the lucky one. Aintcha never eard the words excuse me before?

**Man**    You shouldn't be blocking the stairs. Lift's always out of order so everyone has to use the stairs. And you're blocking them.

**Terry**    That's right ya cunt, I am blockin em. An unless ya say excuse me. An make sure ya use the word please as well, ya aint gettin past, alright?

**Man**    You shouldn't be sitting on the stairs so why should I have to say excuse me? I'm trying to get to my own flat.

**Darren** *stands up and moves away from the step, giving room for the man to pass.*

**Darren**    Ere mate, sorry bout that. Go on ya can walk up. Yer alright.

*Immediately* **Terry** *stands up and holds his hand out to stop the man from passing.*

**Terry**    Wait there mate. (*And to* **Darren**, *with a threatening look.*) Siddown Dal. *Now!* If ud ave wanted ya t' let the cunt past ud a told ya. Siddown.

**Darren** *sits back on the step and* **Terry** *grabs the man by the shoulders and thrusts him against the wall.*

**Terry**    Now listen ya cunt. Did ya ear what I said? Ya say excuse me please. Or ya won't be seein yer flat this side a Christmas. Right?

**Man**   Excuse me please.

**Terry** *lets go of the man and he rushes up the stairs.* **Terry** *looks closely at the step.*

**Terry**   Look at that. Fucker ad filf on is shoes.

**Terry** *takes a tissue from the packet in his pocket and wipes where he's about to sit. He takes the plastic bag from his other pocket, puts the used tissue into it and puts the plastic bag back in his pocket. He sits back down next to* **Darren**.

**Terry**   I ate rude cunts like that.

**Darren**   I fink ya was a bit over the top wiv the geez. Ya terrified im, Tel.

**Terry**   E was a rude cunt!

**Darren**   Right, well like it's nice t' see ya an ave a chat like an all that. But I gotta go, mate. Oh, an it aint never worf waitin fer the lift ere, Tel.

**Terry**   An I bin standin waitin fer it like a cunt. Fuck the fuckin lift in this block. Ow long ya all been buyin off fick-Al? I fort e fucked all is chances wiv is suppliers.

**Darren**   I dunno, Tel. Listen I gotta go mate.

**Darren** *stands up.*

**Terry**   What's up wiv ya Dal? Siddown!

*Reluctantly* **Darren** *sits back down.*

**Terry**   I asked ya a question, expect an answer. Or perhaps ya fancy a fuckin slap.

**Darren**   Dun talk t' me like that, Tel, we're mates frum way back. Ain't right ya talkin t' me like that.

**Terry**   Wadya expect? Sounds like that cunt, fick-Al's yer best mate now.

**Darren**   E aint my best mate, Tel. But I aint got nuffink gainst im.

**Terry** Well I never liked im. Not only is e fick as shit, e's a lyin cunt as well. E's got no loyalties, no respect an is fuckin deals'r always shit.

**Darren** I know is deals are shit. But fer us in the block it's andy when e's got.

**Terry** Well ow long's e ad fer?

**Darren** Maybe two, free weeks. Somefink like that. E come inta sum cash an bought alf ounce. First lump e's been able t' buy in awhile.

**Terry** Come inta sum cash eh? Ooh's e gettin the gear frum?

**Darren** Why ya askin me that? I dunno, Tel.

**Terry** Dal, I asked ya ooh e's gettin the fuckin gear frum. Ooh's sellin t' im?

**Darren** Oh Tel, fer fuck's sake. I dunno.

**Terry** Dal, I ain't got time t' be talkin pleasantries all fuckin day. Yer the last person I wanna ave a bull an cow wiv so dun fuck me bout.

**Darren** I jus dunno where e's gettin the gear frum. Straight up, Tel. What difference does it make anyway?

**Terry** *leans forward and puts his hands round* **Darren**'s *throat.* **Darren** *answers immediately.*

**Darren** The Turks, Tel. Alright, e's gettin it frum the fuckin Turks down The Old Kent.

**Terry** *takes his hands away from* **Darren**'s *throat.*

**Terry** Sorry bout that, Dal. Why didn'tcha find me an tell me Ficko was sellin good gear?

**Darren** E told all of us in the block t' say nuffink t' no one.

**Terry** Dal, um gettin very un'appy ere mate. Is that what the fick cunt said? Tell me the trufe. What loyalty ya got t' that fick prat?

**Darren**   E did say that. But e also said t' make double sure it never got back t'cha in particular. E ain't that bad, Tel. Ya know e's only twenty-one.

**Terry**   Squaddies are killin people when they're eigh-een. Ya know what, Dal?

**Darren**   No, Tel, what?

**Terry**   Every time uv ever bin t' this poxy block lift ain't workin. And now I gotta walk up six floors. If I needed that sorta exercise ud a joined a poncy gym.

**Darren**   Lift's always outa order, Tel. Everyone ooh uses the block knows that.

**Terry**   Oh do they? Well, I ate comin round ere, t' this area, this block. The likes a Ficko, kids like im movin in. No class, mate. Glad I fucked off. Where ya off t' anyway?

**Darren**   I was goin t' get a rock.

**Terry**   Still love a rock, eh?

**Darren**   Yeah. You?

**Terry**   I keep away frum em. Make me act weird. Bita sniff now an again that's ok.

**Darren**   Ere, I know ya ain't come over frum Deptford t' ave a friendly cuppa wiv fick-Al. What's up?

**Terry**   Ficko ain't said nuffink?

**Darren**   No.

**Terry**   Well, me uncle clued me up bout this couple oo was goin way fer a weekend. Never switch their alarm on cos a the cats in the ouse. No cameras an e reckoned there was rich pickins t' be ad. Got in easy an walked out wiv sum beau-iful Georgian silver, a load a Yank money an twen-ee grand a nifties. In an out. So I smoke a bita weed, sniff two long lines an now um in a blindin mood feelin right mella. On top a the world. Um on the lower road at Deptford an suddenly I see

im, fick-Al, by the side a the road an um prayin e dun see me.
Um tryin t' keep me ead down but the arseole's got eyes like
an awk. E spots me an starts wavin an shoutin. Ere can ya
Adam an Eve it? Um loaded down wiv readies, got a pilla-
case full a antique silver in the boot an e's screamin an
shoutin in the middle a the fuckin igh street. Gotta stop the
motor before the ole a Deptford nick are rushin out t' see
what's goin on. Next fing cunt's in the motor tellin me bout is
muvver dyin an e ain't gotta penny fer the funeral. I couldn't
b'lieve it. Shall . . . dead. She's only a cupla years older than
me. I felt right sorry fer im an give im a monkey. E swore on
is dad's life e'd pay me back. I can't b'lieve what a cunt I was
t' b'lieve im. But I mean, ooh's gonna lie an say yer muvver's
brown bread when she aint? Then a cupla days later um
watchin Spurs on the telly. Got a bottle on em t' beat Arsenal
but course they fuckin lose. S' I fancy a Ruby t' get over it an
I find meself in the Indian down the Elephant. Um in there
an some geez I know walks in. Can't stand im as it goes. Right
fat cunt e is. Anyway, e starts talkin t' me. Got a mouf like the
Roverive tunnel e as. An e tells me e see Shall bout five
minutes before e come inta the shop. An e was avin a good ol
natter wiv er. Well, Dal, when I eard that I was very upset.
Very put out, I was, Dal, I can tell ya.

**Darren**   I betcha was, Tel. I can't b'lieve e told ya is muvver
was dead, that's a cuntish fing t' say. (*Beat.*) Ya obviously
never knew is dad died not that long back. Can't remember
when it was exact . . .

**Terry**   Is dad's dead?

**Darren**   Yeah, e walked t' the far enda the platform at
London Bridge. Jumped in front of an incomin train.
Evenin rush-hour. I was on a train jus outside the station on
me way ome frum Honor Oak t' London Bridge. Me train
was eld up fer free hours all cos a is fuckin dad. But sayin
Shall's dead, terrible fing t' say. I tell ya what. Shall's gotta
great body, not a bad looker. I wooden mind givin er one
meself.

**Terry**   I know Shall well, dun I? When Ficko still lived at
ome I made a play fer er. She knocked me back, told me
Ficko said I was a bad'un an t' gimme a miss. E was a orrible
cunt even then. Now she only likes big-time-Charley-Potata
types.

**Darren**   Yeah, yeah. Well, fick-Al told me e won a monkey
on a footie bet. When's e supposed t' pay ya back?

**Terry**   Enda the monf. An uv come t' see ow much e's got
fer me now.

**Darren**   Ok, look um goin. Remember e's a kid.
Ficko's okay.

**Terry** (*raising his voice*)   E ain't ok, t' me e's nuffink but a
fuckin worfless lyin prick.

**Darren**   E can be a bit of a prick sometimes. Anyway, Tel,
good t' see ya but I gotta get off. Pop by soon an we'll go fer
a drink down the Clyde.

**Terry**   Gawd, I aint been there in ages.

**Darren**   Be like ol times, mate.

**Terry**   Mmm, yeah, yeah. We'll go fer a drink an a bit of a
chit-chat an that, eh?

**Darren**   Sure fing, Tel. Anyway, gotta be on me way
mate. Laters.

**Terry**   Yeah, laters me ol fruit-gum.

**Darren** *stands and starts to walk away. He stops and turns towards*
**Terry** *who is just about to start walking up the stairs.*

**Darren**   Tel.

**Terry** *stops and looks towards* **Darren**.

**Darren**   Errrhh, errrrhh . . .I jus wanted t' say like. Like ya
know, go easy on the kid cos e's . . .

**Terry**   Wadya fink um gonna do?

**Darren**    Nuffink, Tel. Um jus sayin like . . .

**Terry**    Dal, Dal. On yer way mate.

**Darren** *nods his head and turns and walks off and* **Terry** *starts walking up the stairs.*

*Lights dim, act closes.*

# Act Two

**Alan** *is curled up asleep on the settee with his clothes on. A packet of Jaffa cakes and a bottle of Coke are on the table. We hear a slight noise at the door, it opens and* **Terry** *walks in. Tip-toeing over to* **Alan**, *he leans down and shouts right next to his head.*

**Terry**   Oyyyyyyy. Oyyyy . . . Ficko.

**Alan** *wakes up with a massive start and lifts his head.*

**Alan**   Oh fuck . . . oh fuckin ell. It's you, Tel.

**Terry**   Right first time, Ficko.

**Alan** *sits up and rubs his eyes.*

**Alan**   Fuck, Tel, ya gimme a right fright.

**Terry**   Ahhh, did I? What a shame.

**Alan**   I weren't expectin no one.

**Terry**   Weren'tcha?

**Alan**   Not really, Tel, no I weren't.

**Terry**   Fink we'll ave a bita music on. Bita background like.

**Terry** *gets out his mobile and puts music on. He lays his phone on the table and random music plays on very low volume. He sits in the armchair.*

**Alan**   Ere, Tel, ow'd ya get in?

**Terry**   I jus appen t' be a drummer, Ficko. Though ya aint gotta be a master feef t' get in this drum. I used a credit card ya stupid fuck.

**Alan**   I lost me keys; that's why I dun use the mortice. I use a card meself t' get in. Keep an old card under the mat outside the door, I do.

**Terry**  Yeah, d' ya? Very secure that is, mate. That's the
sorta security any respectable drug dealer'd be proud of. Ya
know what, Ficko, jus t' see ya uv walked up six flights.

**Alan**  That's nice a ya, Tel. But the fing is I gotta go out.
Um at probation this mornin.

**Terry**  Um a nice fella Ficko. What time ya meant t' be at
probation?

**Alan**  Errrrhhh, fink it's eleven.

**Terry**  Well tough shit it's way after leven. Yuv fucked yer
appointment, mate.

**Alan**  Ave I?

**Terry**  Yeah ya ave.

**Alan** *picks up the packet of Jaffa cakes.*

**Alan**  Ud offer ya one, Tel, but there's only one left in
the packet.

**Terry**  Jaffa cakes are me favourite. I love em. They're the
only sweet fing I eat.

**Alan**  But I only got one left, Tel. I saved it frum last night
t' ave as me breakfast wiv a Coke. I can give ya sum crisps.
Got plenty a them. Or I got anuvver Coke ya can ave.

**Terry**  Ull ave the Jaffa cake. Um the guest.

**Terry** *holds his hand out for* **Alan** *to give him the packet with the
one Jaffa cake in.*

**Terry**  Let's ave it then.

**Alan**  But no one ever gives their last Jaffa cake away, Tel.

**Terry**  Well then this'll be a first won't it, Ficko?

**Alan**  But I only got the one.

**Terry**  Fer fuck's sake. Dya ave t' repeat yerself?

**Alan** No Tel. But I was really lookin forward t' that last one as me breakfast.

**Terry** Was ya?

**Alan** Yeah, I was.

**Terry** What a fuckin shame. Now gimme the biscuit will ya?

*Reluctantly* **Alan** *gives* **Terry** *the packet and he eats the last Jaffa cake.*

**Terry** Mmmm, lovely that was Ficko. Ta very.

**Alan** *goes to the cupboard at the bottom of the shelving unit and takes out two packets of crisps. He returns to the settee and sits down to eat the crisps and drink the Coke.*

**Alan** Want sum crisps?

**Terry** No yer alright. That Jaffa cake filled the ole jus fine.

*As he talks* **Alan** *eats his crisps, and takes an occasional swig of Coke.*

**Alan** Tel, dya mind if I ask ya somefink?

**Terry** Depends what ya wanna ask dunnit.

**Alan** Can ya not call me Ficko. No one calls me that t' me face. An I aint *that* fick, Tel.

**Terry** Oh yeah ya'are. In fact yer ficker than that. Ow dya fink ya got yer nickname, well suited. An when yer as fick as ya are yud never realise ow fick ya was. Wood ya?

**Alan** Not sure I know wotcha mean, Tel.

**Terry** Exactly what um talkin bout Ficko. Anyway, why dya fink um ere?

**Alan** Dunno, Tel.

**Terry** Ya dunno why um ere eh?

**Alan** Not really, no.

**Terry**  I fink ya do mate. I fink even a ficko like ya wood ave sum kinda clue what um doin ere. But t' save beatin bout the bush fer the next cupla ours, ull tell ya that uv come t' ave a little chat wiv ya. But first off, I wanna offer me condolences.

**Alan**  Condolences, Tel?

**Terry**  Yeah, Mister cunt, condolences. Dya know what condolences are?

**Alan**  Errrr, sorta.

**Terry**  What are they then?

**Alan**  Errrr, aint sure I can explain.

**Terry**  Well t' put it plain, I come t' offer me sympafies bout yer mum dyin premature. An I ad t' walk up six flights t' do it.

**Alan**  Look Tel, um sorry bout that wiv me ma, I really am. I feel real bad I said that, onest I do. But ya told me yud ad a touch an five undred quid want much fer ya. Ya wooden a gimme the monkey if I adn't made up that story bout me ma.

**Terry**  Ya know what, Al?

**Alan**  No, Tel, what?

**Terry**  Yer a right cunt, that's what. Talkin boutcha ma bein dead. By rights ya should be feelin me fist in yer face mate. Free days before the enda the monf, uv come round t' see ow yer doin. T' make sure ya know I want that monkey back. No messin mate. That's the monkey ya got on false pretences, Ficko.

**Alan**  Um gettin it all togever, Tel, onest. But I was gonna ask ya if I could make it the enda the week. Give us till Friday, mate, an ull ave the lot fer ya by then.

**Terry**   Listen t' what um tellin ya. Enda the week as far as yer concerned is Wensdee. Ow much ya got fer me now, Ficko?

**Alan**   I ain't got nuffink, serious, Tel. There aint no readies in the drum.

**Terry**   Ow about ya go ask yer dad t' lend it t'cha.

**Alan**   Me dad?

**Terry**   Yeah, yer fuckin dad. Ya know, the dad ooze life ya swore on.

**Alan**   E ain't got no money t' lend me, Tel.

**Terry**   Ow'd ya know that?

**Alan**   I asked im.

**Terry**   Ya asked im did ya?

**Alan**   Yeah, Tel, I asked im. But e aint got none e can gimme.

**Terry**   Is that right? So it weren't yer dad ooh was the jumper. I eard e eld up a cupla undred fousand commuters at London Bridge station by takin a slow stroll in front of a fast-movin train. Ficko, ya got any readies fer me now mate?

**Alan**   No, Tel, straight, I aint. An um sorry bout that wiv me dad.

**Terry**   Bout sorry! Yer jus such a wanker. Ya fink everyone's as fick as you. An ya expect me t' b'lieve ya aint got no readies, nuffink. Wadya fink I am, eh? Some kinda bollockin idiot like you? Ya got gear ain'tcha?

**Alan**   I got a bita personal saved frum last night. Maybe nuff fer one it. But it's already in a works, Tel. Ull share alf wiv ya. I got a new works ya can use.

**Terry**   Well, fank ya s' much. Dal said the gear's strong. Is it?

**Alan**   Dal said?

**Terry**    Yeah, Dal said.

**Alan** (*With a puzzled expression.*)    Mmmm, well it is yeah. But we're sharin what ud ave ad on me own. Yul still feel it though.

**Alan** *gets a syringe filled with brown liquid from the cupboard at the bottom of the shelving unit. After transferring half of the contents into a second syringe he gives it to* **Terry**.

**Alan**    Ya got a cig, Tel?

**Terry**    Dun smoke do I?

**Alan**    Oh yeah, yeah. Fuck. Smoked me last one last night. Was gonna get a single this mornin t' go wiv me it.

**Terry**    Oh yeah, was ya?

**Alan**    I was yeah. Gotta ave a cig wiv an it aintcha?

**Terry**    Is that right? Well even if ya ad one ya wooden be smokin it round me mate.

**Alan**    Oh right, ok, Tel. Ere, I use a belt. It's the only fing I got. Ya wanna use it first?

**Terry**    I dun need no tourni. I got good veins, mate. Get it first time. Always.

**Terry** *picks up his phone and changes the track. After increasing the volume slightly he places it back on the table. 'Golden Brown' by The Stranglers plays.* **Alan** *gets a leather belt from under the cushion on the settee. He ties it round his upper arm and sits down.* **Terry** *takes his jacket off and rolls up his shirt sleeve. He has his fix standing and then dabs the blood on his arm with a tissue from his pocket. Placing the cap back on the syringe he looks around for somewhere to dispose of it.*

**Terry**    Wadya do wiv yer used works?

**Alan**    I frow em in the bin.

**Terry**    Dya put the cap back on before ya frow em?

**Alan**    'Course.

*Terry goes over to the pedal bin and opens it. He looks closely at the contents.*

**Terry**    Well aint that strange. There aint a single needle in ere mate. Dya frow em out the winda d'ya?

**Alan**    No Tel.

**Terry**    When I leave ere I'll be takin a look in the grass under the winda. Ya sure ya aint chucked no needles out the winda?

**Alan**    Yeah, yeah double sure. But maybe Dal might frow is out the winda . . . or it could be Jack or Sam.

**Terry**    Is that right?

**Alan**    Dunno, Tel, but could be.

**Terry**    Yeah the moon *could* be shaped like a cunt but it aint.

*Terry throws his needle and the tissue in the pedal bin. Then he rolls down his sleeve, puts his jacket back on and sits back down on the armchair and sings along whilst moving his body to the music.*

**Alan**    Ere, Tel. Any chance yud get this vein fer me. It's easier if someone else does it.

**Terry**    Fuck off ya cunt. Ooh dya fink I am, Florence fuckin Nightingale? Get it yerself.

**Alan**    Alright, no prob, Tel, ull get it meself.

*As **Terry** gets more into the music and moves his body about and sings along **Alan** fixes himself sitting. After dabbing the blood using the bottom of his t-shirt he puts the cap on the syringe, stands and throws it in the bin then sits back down on the settee. **Terry** picks up his phone and decreases the volume to barely audible. He places it back on the table. (When 'Golden Brown' ends random music plays.)*

**Alan**    Wadya reckon on the gear?

**Terry**    Ardly felt it. But it'll do. Dya know what, Ficko?

**Alan**   No. What?

**Terry**   Before I come up ere I was talkin t' Dal fer awhile downstairs. An e mentioned ya was sellin gear t' the ole block. Probly means yer sellin t' the ole a Souf London. An yer tellin me ya ain't got no money. An the only gear ya got is what's in the works.

**Alan**   Ere Tel, ow bout I work down me debt a bit by comin out wiv ya t' work like?

**Terry**   Work down yer debt, bollocks. Dya onestly fink ud ave a twenty-one-year-old muggy cunt like ya workin wiv *me*. Where ya gettin yer gear, Ficko?

**Alan**   Off a bunch a Pakis in New Cross.

**Terry**   Pakis? In New Cross!!? Pakis, eh?

**Alan**   Yeah, there's Pakis in New Cross, Tel.

**Terry**   I know there's bound t' be Pakis in New fuckin Cross. There's Pakis everwhere ya cunt. But there ain't none sellin gear in New Cross.

**Alan**   I dun fink ya know everyone ooh's sellin gear in New Cross, Tel.

**Terry**   Well that's where yer wrong. I fink I do. Anyway, yer best mate, Dal, e said ya was gettin it off the fuckin Captain Kirks.

**Alan**   Ooh's the fuckin Captain Kirks, Tel?

**Terry**   Ain'tcha never watched *Star Trek*?

**Alan**   Yeah, I see one a the films. I know ooh Captain Kirk is. But I dunno what Dal's talkin bout sayin I got it frum the fuckin Captain Kirks. Ooh the fuck are the fuckin Captain Kirks?

**Terry**   The fuckin Turks, ya dim-shit.

**Alan**   Oh right, the Turks. I aint never eard that one before.

**Terry**   Well now ya ave. An ave ya bin gettin the gear off the Turks?

**Alan**   I can't give away me sources can I mate? Ya got a mobile number I can ave?

**Terry**   I dun give me number out t' no one. Me, I do all me business face-t'-face.

**Terry** *gets up from the armchair, stands next to* **Alan** *and peers down at him.*

**Terry**   Ficko, I asked ya wever ya was gettin the gear off the Captain Kirks.

**Alan**   Yeah, Tel, yeah yeah, I ave, I ave bin gettin it off em.

**Terry** *sits back down.*

**Terry**   I fort ya was taboo wiv everyone ooh's sellin. Ow come them Turks'r sellin tya? I might jus go round an ask em if they'll sell t' me direct, cut you right out the picture. Get me personal at cost.

**Alan**   They won't sell t' ya, Tel.

**Terry**   If they bin sellin t' ya they'll sell t' me mate.

**Alan**   They won't, Tel. Ya need an in wiv this bunch an I know the ead oncho. E goes wiv me ma, shaggin er regular. That's why is firm's sellin t' me.

**Terry**   Talkin boutcha ma like that. First she's dead. Then she's shaggin. Yer a kid's got no respect fer no one. Well um tellin ya, Ficko, dun treat me like a cunt. Be a mistake. A very big mistake. Make sure yer round me drum wiv a monkey by Wensdee. An if ya aint ull come lookin fer ya.

**Alan**   Oh, dun worry, Tel, ull be there mate.

**Terry**   Oh . . . an ull expect ya before twelve. An that's twelve noon not twelve midnight.

*Lights dim, act closes.*

## Act Three

*Tuesday evening,* **Alan***'s flat.* **Alan** *and* **Darren** *are sitting on the settee. On the table are an ashtray, two empty hypodermic syringes, a tablespoon with a filter and brown residue on it, a packet of cigarettes, a lighter and a box of vitamin C powder. Radio 1 plays softly in the background.* **Darren** *and* **Alan** *are smoking. (When their cigarettes finish they stub them out in the ashtray and don't smoke again during the act.)*

**Alan**  That's ace gear, that, init Dal? Ya really feel it.

**Darren**  Ya say that every time um ere mate. Be a lot better if ya wasn't rippin everyone off on the weight.

**Alan**  Ya mus fink the deals'r ok or ya wooden be up ere buyin.

**Darren**  The deals aint ok but it's convenient. Aint gotta leave the block ave I?

*A knock on the door. We hear a slight noise (as she unlocks the door with a credit card) and* **Rebecca** *walks in.*

**Darren**  Right Becks?

**Rebecca**  Yeah, good.

**Rebecca** *sits in the armchair.*

**Alan**  Right Becks?

**Rebecca**  Yeah um alright Al.

**Alan**  Ya need gear?

**Rebecca**  No I dun. Jus socialisin. Been at me mum's aint I? Got a score's worf yesdee an anuvver one this mornin on er estate. Double what ud get off ya fer a score.

**Alan**  No way no one's sellin double what I sell fer a score.

**Rebecca**   Was a proper alf gee. Yud sooner slit yer froat than give a proper alf fer a score.

**Darren** (*To* **Rebecca**.)   When I never see ya last night I fort ya was gonna be stayin at yer ma's all week. Fort ya ad the ump.

**Rebecca**   I never ad the ump, Dal. But as it goes I *was* gonna stay all week. Only I changed me mind. Is that ok?

**Darren**   It's ok. But next time ask me first.

**Rebecca**   Oh, fuck off, Dal. Yer such a wanker.

**Alan**   Do ya know what Becks? Dal only told Tel I was sellin gear. An e come up ere an was very (*Beat.*) fretenin.

**Rebecca**   I wondered what Tel was doin ere yesdee.

**Darren** (*To* **Rebecca**.)   Yeah well after ya left us me an Tel was talkin fer ages. E starts tellin me bout ow e borra'd Al a monkey. An in the course of our conversation it just sorta slipped out that Al was dealin.

**Alan**   Why dya ave t' say somefink?

**Darren**   E was comin t' see ya anyway.

**Rebecca**   I still dun fink ya shoulda told Tel that Al was dealin.

**Darren** (*To* **Rebecca**.)   Did ya ear what I said? Al leant a monkey off Tel an e's meant t' ave it paid back by the enda the monf. That's tomorra. That's what e come t' see Al about. An Al only got the readies off Tel cos e said is muvver was brown bread.

**Rebecca**   Ya never said yer muvver was dead didya? Tell us ya never said that?

**Alan**   Look, me muvver ain't dead an she ain't gonna die jus cos I said she was dead.

**Rebecca**   Ohhh, that's so fuckin low, mate. Why'd ya say that?

**Alan**   Oh shut up bout it. Look, ya forget that evenin when we was all sat ere moanin. No one could get no small deals nowhere an all we ad was meff. But if ud ave ad a monkey I coulda gone straight out an bought alf ounce a pucker gear. Then I sell the gear fer a little profit. Then I buy the next lot. That was me finkin. So the very next day um scratchin round in Deptford an I see im, Tel, in is motor. Soon as e sees me e's wavin like mad an shoutin out the winda tryin t' get me attention. E stops the motor an I walk over. E was cagey, wooden tell me what e'd done but says e's ad a right touch. S' e gives me a lift back t' Bermondsey an as e's drivin e's talkin t' me like um is best mate. Um finkin should I ask im fer sum readies. But I know e wooden gimme me the drippins frum is nose, im. So t' get sum sympafy the only fing I can fink of is t' say me muvver died.

**Rebecca**   Jus can't b'lieve ya said that.

**Alan**   Oh shut up goin on bout it now, bofe a ya. Yer lucky I got gear an ya can get it s' easy. Ere, do us a favour. Go down the offy an gemme a packet a Jaffa cakes.

**Rebecca**   Are ya kiddin? Dun even eat em.

**Alan**   Will ya go down the offy fer me, Dal?

**Darren**   What's it worf?

**Alan**   Give ya one for goin.

**Darren**   Gimme two an ull fink bout it.

**Alan**   Nah, one's all ull give ya.

**Darren**   Then go fuck yerself.

**Alan** *leaves the flat.*

**Rebecca**   Dya fink Tel'll come ere tomorra?

**Darren**   If Ficko aint round is drum wiv sum readies e'll be ere.

**Rebecca**   I might come ere tomorra mornin then.

**Darren**   Why wood ya do that?

**Rebecca**   Well ya never know what Tel'll do, d' ya?

**Darren**   Wooden like t' fink what Tel'll do if Ficko dun pay that money back. We're talkin bout Goose ere.

**Rebecca**   Wotcha talkin bout?

**Darren**   Goose. I told ya.

**Rebecca**   Told me what? I dunno wotcha talkin bout, Goose!

**Darren**   Bollocks! Me fuckin memory. I fort I told ya, coulda sworn I told ya.

**Rebecca**   Well ya never. Ya never told me nuffink, s' tell me.

**Darren**   Well, I was wiv Ficko an we was well out of it. An we was tryin t' come up wiv a nickname fer Tel. Ya know e likes a bita rymin slang. So um finkin like, ya know 'Screw-Loose' gotta be 'Goose' aint it?

**Rebecca**   Oh no! That was a *big* mistake inventin a name like that in fronta Al.

**Darren**   Well, I know that dun I? Was out me ead an sorta finkin out loud. 'Course, I told Ficko never t' use that nickname fer Tel t' no one like.

**Rebecca**   Trufe is I feel a bit sorry fer Al.

**Darren**   Can't understand why ya always feel sorry fer im. Ardly no one'll deal wiv im cos a is antics. An e knows Tel dun like im so e should never ave lent money off im.

**Rebecca**   But e's young aint e. Always gettin imself inta a mess, reminds me a me bruv.

**Darren**   Yer bruv was in a gang an e got stabbed cos e was bein flash t' the wrong people.

**Rebecca**   E never deserved t' die did e?

**Darren**   No, course he never. But it aint nuffink like the situation Ficko's in.

**Rebecca**    Me bruv was just a kid.

**Darren**    Ere, it aint that ya fancy Ficko is it?

**Rebecca**    No it aint. But even if I did it's got nuffink t' do wiv ya as it?

**Darren**    Tell me there aint nuffink goin on between ya two.

**Rebecca**    I aint gotta tell ya shit.

**Darren**    S' it's true then?

**Rebecca**    If ya mus know . . . it aint.

**Darren**    I dun give a fuck anyway. Ya used t' fancy Tel an that never bovvered me.

**Rebecca**    That was before the accident. An not much it didn't bovver ya. Ya kept on askin me an askin me, never let up. An when I told ya, ya sulked like a baby.

**Darren**    No, I never.

**Rebecca**    Oh shut up, Dal.

**Alan** *walks back in munching on a Jaffa cake and holding the packet.*

**Alan**    Was the last packet they ad in the offy.

**Darren**    Wiv ya buyin em daily, ardly surprisin. Ya gonna gimme one?

**Alan**    Why should I? Ya wooden go an get em.

**Darren**    Greedy fuck. Look mate, yer in trouble. Ya must ave sumfink t' give Tel back.

**Alan**    Nuffink worf talkin bout.

**Darren**    So ow come the little story never come true? Ya lend a monkey, buy the gear an sell it at a profit. Ya got alf ounce. Even wiv yer own abit ya gotta get back a carpet profit at least. Then ya pay the monkey back an use the profit t' buy yer next lot.

**Alan**  Is your carpet free undred or firty?

**Darren**  Free undred.

**Alan**  Right, well I reckon I made more than a free-er. But I done all that an a fair bita the monkey on rocks. I never ad nuff t' buy me next alf an I only bought a quarter this time cos I only ad free undred left.

**Rebecca**  Al, yer in deep shit.

**Darren**  Yer tellin me ya aint got nuffink t' give im?

**Alan**  Might be able t' get a longun t'gever by tomorra but that'd leave me short on the next quarter.

**Darren**  Fuck the next quarter. That's the last fing ya gotta worry bout cos I doubt yul be dealin much longer. Ya dun realise what serious trouble yer in.

**Rebecca**  Ya know Tel ain't bin right since the accident, Dal. What if e loses it?

**Darren**  Then Al'll be brown bread like is muvver. An like is farver. E won't ave t' worry bout payin no monkey back.

**Alan**  Dun say fings like that, Dal, that's fuckin orrible, mate.

**Darren**  Oh, shut up.

**Rebecca** (*To* **Darren**.)  Ya know Tel well frum way back. Can't ya go round talk t' im, smoove fings over?

**Darren**  Dya know what appened yesdee, Becks? When I wooden say ooh Al was gettin the gear frum, Tel puts is ands round me froat. An um finkin wood e really strangle me if I dun tell im?

**Alan**  An wadya do?

**Darren**  Wadya fink I done. I fuckin told im a course.

**Alan**  Ya took a right liberty tellin im that. Even if ya never told im e'd never a strangled ya. Wood e Dal? E wooden a actually done it?

**Darren**  Ooh knows. I wooden put nuffink past im.

**Rebecca**    Dal, ya know Tel better than anyone. What's the best solution fer Al?

**Darren**    There aint one if e dun pay them readies back. (*To* **Alan**.) Maybe leave London mate.

**Alan**    Fuck off, Dal. I aint leavin London jus cos I owe a monkey. Tel can fuckin it me. Won't be the first time uv took a whack. E aint gonna kill me fer a monkey, is e?

**Darren**    Well look what appened at Micky's.

**Rebecca**    Forgot bout that.

**Alan**    Ooh's Micky?

**Darren**    Tel's bruv.

**Alan**    Tell us what appened then.

**Darren**    Well, we was sittin round Micky's drum. Me, Micky an Tel all normal sorta fing, avin a quiet friendly drink. Bita talkin, lotta laughin, when suddenly outa the blue Tel gets up off the couch an starts lookin up at the ceilin. Is face sorta contorts. (**Darren** *contorts his face to emphasise what he is saying about* **Terry**.) E stays like that fer a few seconds. Then e says t' Micky, 'Ya fink I dunno ya bin talkin bad bout me but I do see.' Micky dunno what's goin on an e looks at me all sorta puzzled like. But I dunno what's app'nin eever. Then Tel sits down like nuffink appened an we carry on talkin. Micky finks it's a joke but I aint s' sure. Then a few minutes later Tel stands up an looks at the ceilin again. Is face contorts an next fing e's got is hands round Micky's froat. An e's stranglin im. Like e wants t' kill im. Is own bruv. Um screamin at im. Stop, stop. I grab is arms. But e's too strong. Um fuckin frantic, mate. I can't do nuffink. An Micky's startin t' gurgle. Then suddenly it's like Tel wakes up. E releases is grip frum Micky's froat an stops. E'd gone back t' normal, jus like that. E couldn't say enough sorrys. But poor ole Micky, what a state e was in. Ere, Tel weren't lookin too clever eever. E was slumped in the armchair lookin green.

**Alan**   Oh fuck.

**Rebecca**   What we gonna do then?

**Darren**   Wadya mean, what *we* gonna do? I aint gonna do nuffink. It's Al's problem.

**Rebecca**   If ya stay wiv Al tomorra mornin, Dal, Tel won't do nuffink bad.

**Darren**   Wotcha talkin bout, Becks? I jus bin tellin ya when Tel tried t' kill is own bruv an I was there then. An yesdee mornin e went fer a geez on the stairs an I was there. No way will I be ere tomorra.

**Rebecca**   Ya can't jus do nuffink, Dal.

**Darren**   Ya stay ere wiv im then if ya wanna.

**Alan**   Will ya wait wiv me tomorra, Becks? E won't do nuffink bad if yer ere.

**Rebecca**   I dunno Al. Ull ave t' fink bout it.

**Alan**   Go on, Becks. There's no way e'd do somefink bad if yer ere.

**Darren**   Dun do it, Becks. Um tellin ya. Tel's dangerous. E ain't never liked Al. Now e's really gonna ave the ravin ump wiv im. An if yer ere it'll wind Tel up more.

**Alan**   Take no notice, Becks. If ya speak up fer me t' Tel, ull always do ya good deals.

**Rebecca**   Bit late in the day init?

**Darren**   Ya know what, Al? Tel's right boutcha. Ya jus aint a nice kid. (*To* **Rebecca**.) Honest, stay way frum ere tomorra. E aint even tryin t' elp imself s' what ya tryin fer? Laters, Becks. Besta luck, Al.

**Darren** *exits and* **Rebecca** *stands to leave.*

**Alan**   See ya tomorra mornin Becks? Becks . . .

*Lights dim, act closes.*

## Act Four

*Wednesday morning around noon. **Alan**'s lounge. On the table are a Coke and a packet of Jaffa cakes. **Alan** is sitting on the settee munching the biscuits and drinking Coke while heavy drum and bass music plays faintly in the background. **Rebecca** walks in and sits in the armchair.*

**Rebecca**   Alright, Al?

**Alan**   Iya, Becks.

**Rebecca**   I ope yuv got sum money fer Tel.

**Alan**   I aint. I needed sum gear. Was runnin low. Fort I might as well buy anuvver quarter. Got it late last night after ya an Dal left. Only jus made the free undred.

**Rebecca**   What!? Ya gotta be crazy? Tel'll be ere an ya aint got a penny fer im. Yul ave t' give im the quarter. Try t' get im t' take that fer now.

**Alan**   I aint got a full quarter left. An I need it s' I aint givin it t' im.

**Rebecca**   Wotcha need is yer ead examined, that's wotcha need. Ya aint takin fings serious enough, Al. What's wrong wiv ya?

**Alan**   What's e gonna do while yer ere, eh? I reckon e'll clump me. Then ull plead wiv im an buy sum time. Um good at talkin me way outa fings.

**Rebecca**   Was ya even listenin t' what Dal was sayin last night? Bout Micky. An ow he was gonna strangle Dal jus cos e wooden say ooh ya was buyin off?

**Alan**   Yeah course I was list-nin. But the fing is e never. An I fink Dal exapperates.

**Rebecca**   E what?

**Alan**    Ya know, e makes fings bigger than they are.

**Rebecca**    Ya mean e exaggerates.

**Alan**    Yeah that's it, that's what e does. An as mad as ya an Dal say Tel is, e aint never killed no one. An e aint gonna kill me fer a monkey. E aint gettin me gear an that's it.

**Rebecca**    Al, Dal ain't exaggeratin. E was best mates wiv Tel fer years. They grew up t'gever. E only stopped angin round wiv im after the Micky fing. If e says yer in trouble e knows what e's talkin bout. Offer Tel the quarter an then say yul give im a bullseye a week, or somefink.

**Alan**    I aint givin im the quarter an that's it!

**Rebecca**    Alright, Al, ave it yer own way but sorry, I gotta go. I dun like finkin bout what's gonna appen ere. Ya should be doin everyfink in the world possible t' fix fings. But ya aint doin nuffink. Um goin.

**Alan**    No Becks; dun go. Stay ere. Ull give ya a joey fer nuffink.

**Rebecca**    A poxy tenner's worfa gear. Jeez what am I doin ere?

**Rebecca** *stands to leave.*

**Alan**    Dun go Becks. If yer ere ya can speak up fer me. Um sure ya can keep im off me back.

**Rebecca**    Al, ya won't elp yerself so I can't elp ya. See ya.

*As* **Rebecca** *walks towards the front door* **Terry** *walks in carrying a doctor's leather holdall.*

*From hereon* **Terry** *remains standing, moving round the room the whole time.*

**Terry**    Becks!!? Never expected t' see ya ere girl. I ad everyfink planned out. Now, ya bein ere, that's confused me a bit. Wotcha doin ere girl?

**Rebecca**    Well . . . errrhh . . . errhh, see like I jus sorta popped up t' say ello an that. An I was errhh . . . I was jus bout t' go, Tel, as it appens.

**Terry**    Was ya? Siddown a minute.

**Rebecca**    But I was jus bout t' . . .

**Terry**    Jus siddown fer a minute will ya.

**Rebecca** *sits on the settee.*

**Terry**    Ere, wadya finka this Becks? Nice init?

**Terry** *holds his leather doctor's holdall out.*

**Rebecca**    Yeah, is.

**Terry**    Some litte toe-rag tea-leaf nicked it frum a surgery. I give im two undred moody Bensons fer it. Worf it wanit?

**Rebecca**    Yeah, Tel, was.

**Terry**    Fuckin toe-rag'll *need* a doctor after e smokes them fake fags.

**Terry** *puts the holdall down next to the settee.*

**Terry**    Now Ficko . . . Al, dun say nuffink mate. Move that chair two feet in fronta the shelves an sit on it. Oh wait before ya do that, turn off that shit music. We'll ave my music on.

**Alan** *turns the radio off.* **Terry** *takes his mobile from his pocket, taps the screen a couple of times, puts it on the table and random music plays softly.* **Alan** *picks up the Jaffa cakes and* **Terry** *snatches the packet out of his hands.*

**Terry**    Well ow bout that then. Wud ya b'lieve it eh, only one left. Did ya save this last one fer me, Ficko?

**Alan**    No I never, Tel. I was jus gonna eat it.

**Terry**    Was ya really?

**Alan**    I was, yeah. It's me last one.

**Terry**   I can see that. I always seem t' be ere when yer on yer last one. Aintcha got no more then?

**Alan**   No, I aint.

**Terry**   Tough shit then init.

**Terry** *eats the last Jaffa cake.*

**Terry**   Mmmm, tasty that was. They're always the biz them Jaffa cakes. Now move that chair an go sit where I told ya.

**Terry** *points to the chair he wants moved.*

**Alan**   Why's that, Tel?

**Terry**   Ull tell ya one more time, Ficko. But dun gimme no answer. Dun say nuffink. Move that chair two feet in fronta the shelves an sit on it.

**Alan** *moves the chair in front of the shelves and sits down.*

**Terry**   I said put the chair two feet in front a the shelves. Ya got it touchin em.

**Alan** *stands up and moves the chair forward and then sits back down on it.*

**Terry**   Don'tcha know what two fuckin feet is? Move it forward sum more.

**Alan** *stands and moves the chair forward and sits back down.*

**Terry**   Right, now keep quiet an listen. Oh ang on, nearly forgot. Remember when I was ere a cupla days ago? I told ya I was gonna take a look in the grass below yer winda?

**Alan**   Yeah, sorta remember.

**Terry**   Well guess what? I only found a loada used needles in the fuckin grass, mate. An they never ad their caps on. Dya know anyfink bout that?

**Alan**   No, Tel, no ud never chuck used works out the winda.

**Terry**   Ya sure bout that?

**Alan**  Yeah, deffo, Tel, weren't me.

**Terry**  Becks, does Dal frow is works out the winda?

**Rebecca**  Nah, Tel. I aint never seen im frow a works out the winda.

**Alan**  Like I said, Tel. Could be Jack or Sam.

**Terry**  Ya an yer could be's. Could be fuckin Michaelangelo.

**Alan**  Oo's e?

**Terry**  E's a painter an decorator famous in Greenwich e is. Be sure ull find out bout them needles. Anyway, back to biz. S' Ficko . . .

**Alan**  Tel, can I jus say . . .

**Terry**  (*interrupting and using a menacing voice*)  SHUT IT!! It's well past twelve now. Ya was meant t' be at mine by twelve wiv a monkey. Ya never ad no intention a bringin me me readies didya?

**Alan**  I was gonna come an talk t'ya bout it, Tel, honest I was. But Becks come up an we started talkin an I never realised the time.

**Terry**  Oh right, I see. Is that what appened Becks? Ya come up an stopped Ficko frum bringin me me money?

**Rebecca**  No, Tel, no. I never stopped im.

**Terry**  Ficko, ave ya got me readies?

**Alan**  Not really, Tel, but . . .

**Terry**  (*interrupting*)  Dun say anuvver word till I tell ya. Do not speak. Dun say nuffink. Nod yer ead if ya understand what I jus said.

**Alan**  But Tel, all I wanted t' say. All I wanted t' say was. I might be able t' . . .

**Terry** *slaps* **Alan** *round the face before he can complete the sentence.*

**Rebecca**   NO, Tel, no!!

**Terry**   Shut the fuck up, Becks. Keep outa it an dun
interfere. Now Al, Ficko. Listen carefully this time mate.
Listen very, very carefully. Do not say anuvver fuckin word
unless I give ya permission first. Not one word. Not one
word bout nuffink. Now do not speak. Do *not* interrupt me.
Jus nod yer ead if ya understand what uv jus said t'ya.

**Alan** *nods his head.*

**Terry**   Mazin, well done. I was down Tower Bridge Road
yesdee Ficko. Gettin sum pie an mash I was. See a geez in
there I know. Used t' ang round wiv me an Dal. Good mate
like. Wooden put me wrong. E told me ya bin muggin me
off. Puttin it bout that yud taken me fer a cunt. Ya ad the
fuckin front t' call me Goose t' me mate. E'd never eard that
before. Uv never eard that before. E fort it was funny e did.
Screw-loose-Goose. Spose ya also fink that's funny dya?
Do ya?

**Alan**   No Tel. No Tel, I dun fink that. But it weren't me
ooh . . .

**Terry** (*interrupting and raising his voice*)   Shut it. Jus fuckin
shut it an listen. An then ya told im, me good mate, that ya
got a monkey off me an I was gonna ave t' whistle fer it. Is
that right bright spark?

**Alan**   No, no, Tel. I . . . err, err . . . what I said was . . .

**Terry** *breaks in.*

**Terry**   Ficko . . . Al. Uv warned ya already. Won't warn ya
again. Dun speak. Shake yer ead or nod it. But dun say
nuffink unless I give ya the go a'ead first. Now jus listen.
When I ear that a muggy fick cunt like you is talkin bout me
like *um* a mug . . . callin me names I aint never earda it
irritates me bad, real bad. I can't tell ya jus ow bad it irritates
me. Now Becks, I was jus askin ya what ya was doin ere. Yer
up ere buyin gear aintcha?

**Rebecca**  No Tel. I aint. I got sum gear when I was at me mum's, on er estate. I bin goin there t' get me gear.

**Terry**  So ya dunno if Ficko ere, mister sharp brain, clever bollocks. Wever the lyin fuck's got anyfink then?

**Rebecca**  No, Tel. I dunno.

**Terry**  Ya sure bout that, Becks?

**Rebecca**  Yeah, um sure. I dunno if e's oldin.

**Terry**  Whatcha doin ere then? Ya an Ficko good mates now? Like up ere regular are ya?

**Rebecca**  I wooden say regular, Tel. We live in the same block, we're sorta mates. Sometimes I pop up ere. That sorta mate, Tel. Nuffink special.

**Terry**  Nuffink special eh? Live in the same block sorta mate? An sometimes ya jus appen t' pop up ere d' ya? An ya do buy gear off im don'tcha?

**Rebecca**  Yeah, when e's sellin I do. If the gear's ok. Everyone knows is deals are shit but it's andy im bein upstairs frum me.

**Terry**  Oh very andy. Nice t' ave mates ooh rip ya off livin in the same block as ya init? Jus stay there a bit, girl.

**Rebecca**  But I gotta go, Tel.

**Terry**  Aint no rush, Becks. Fing is this cunt owes me a monkey. E shoulda bin at mine this mornin but e's a lumpa shit. An now e's made me walk up six fuckin flights again. Ere Becks, do us a favour. That one I jus ad's gimme the taste. Can ya go down the shop an gemme a packet a Jaffa cakes please?

**Terry** *takes a five-pound note from his pocket and hands it to* **Rebecca**.

**Rebecca**  Will ya be alright, Tel?

**Terry**  What!!? Ya worried Ficko might attack me?

**Rebecca**   Ardly, Tel. I jus dun want ya t' do nuffink bad.

**Terry**   Nuffink bad!? What's that mean, Becks?

**Rebecca**   Nuffink, Tel. It dun mean nuffink.

**Terry** (*Raising his voice.*)   Why dya say it then?

**Rebecca**   Errrhh, dunno, Tel. Jus like sorta, errr . . . sorta talkin like. Never meant nuffink specific like.

**Terry**   Jus sorta talkin, eh?

**Rebecca**   Yeah, jus sorta talkin. Ya know ya say sumfink. It jus comes out. Ya dun fink ya jus say it.

**Terry**   Dun fink ya jus say it, eh? (*Beat.*) Ya fink um a bad person don'tcha? Cos only bad people do bad fings. Is that right?

**Rebecca**   I aint never given it much fort, Tel.

**Terry**   Didn'tcha jus say ya didn't want me t' do nuffink bad?

**Rebecca**   I did but that dun mean I fink yer a bad person. I only know ya as a mate, Tel. Someone ya see round an get t' know a bit.

**Terry**   But yuv eard bad fings bout me?

**Rebecca**   I jus eard it said ya wasn't a person t' take liber-ies wiv, Tel, that's all.

**Terry**   So ya never eard it said I was a bad person then?

**Rebecca**   Nah, I aint. Nah. Uv eard it said ya aint shy of a ruck an that's it, Tel.

**Terry**   Ok then. Go an gemme those Jaffa cakes please.

**Rebecca**   Yeah sure, ok. See ya in a bit.

**Rebecca** *exits.*

**Alan**   Tel, I gotta speak. It's good news. They finally fixed the lift. Ya never ad t' walk up six flights. If ya listen close ya can ear it. Listen.

**Terry** (*with raised voice*)   WHAT!! Listen to the fuckin lift!? Fuck me, what are ya on mate? An ya reckon that's good news d'ya? I never give ya permission t' speak did I?

**Alan**   Tel, can I ave permission t' speak?

**Terry**   Say please.

**Alan**   Please.

**Terry**   Not jus please. Say, can I ave permission t' speak please.

**Alan**   Can I ave permission t' speak please, Tel?

**Terry**   Maybe. Jus depends what yer gonna say dunit.

**Alan**   Ull give ya the money, Tel. I will. All of it. Jus gimme a little more time. Please, Tel . . .

**Terry** *stares at* **Alan** *and rubs his chin with his hand.*

**Alan**   Tel, ull give ya . . .

**Terry** (*interrupting*)   Ere, Ficko, let's talk a little. D'ya remember when I made a play fer yer ma when ya was still livin at ome?

**Alan**   Nah, dun remember that, Tel.

**Terry**   I fink ya do mate. Ya was bout seven-een. Before me accident.

**Alan**   Long time ago init, Tel?

**Terry**   Only bout four years. Not that long that ya can't remember mate. Is it comin back t' ya yet?

**Alan**   Sorta.

**Terry**   S' ya remember when I had a fing fer yer ma then? An ya told er yud eard bad fings bout me. Remember that?

**Alan**   Kinda.

**Terry**   An cos a them bad fings yud eard bout me, ya said she should gimme a wide berf. What are those bad fings ya eard bout me, Ficko?

**Alan**   Oh, can't remember that, Tel. Four years ago, long time init? Can't fink back *that* far.

**Terry**   Well ya better start tryin or ull prod yer memory a bit. Ow bout that?

**Terry** *reaches into the holdall. He takes out a razor-edge knife and holds it in his hand.*

**Alan**   Oh yeah, yeah it's all comin back t' me now, Tel.

**Terry** *puts the knife down on the table.*

**Terry**   Well?

**Alan**   It weren't nuffink real bad. Jus that ya was a bit andy wiv yer fists. That sorta fing. Marked a few people up.

**Terry**   What sorta people?

**Alan**   Dunno wotcha mean, Tel. What sorta people.

**Terry**   Wadya mean ya dunno what I mean? Did I jus go an pick on people workin in Tesco's an cut em? Or maybe ya eard I never liked the way the shelves was bein stacked, s' I floored a few shelf-fillers. Was that it?

**Alan**   No, I dun fink ya done nuffink like that Tel.

**Terry**   Course I never. The people I done, done somefink t' deserve it.

**Alan**   Yeah Tel.

**Terry**   But because a that ya didn't fink yer ma should go out wiv me eh? Ya fort she was too good fer me.

**Alan**   No, it weren't that, Tel. I sorta exapperated t' me ma boutcha.

**Terry**   Ya what?

**Alan**    Ya know I sorta exapperated. Tried t' make er fink ya was worse than ya was. Like real mean like.Then she'd give ya a miss.

**Terry**    Fer fuck's sake. Ya mean exaggerated. Ya exaggerated not fuckin exabberated.

**Alan**    I never said exabberated, Tel. I said exapperated.

**Terry** (*Raising his voice.*)    Oh fuck what ya said. Ya mean exaggerated.

**Alan**    Yeah that's right, Tel, That's what I mean. I done that. I mean, yer a good-lookin geez, well built an that. Women fancy ya. An I fort me ma might really get t' like ya. Ya know, like special like. An then if ya an er got t'gever proper ya coulda made fings ard fer me t' live there. Like sorta gimme discipline like. I was finkin bout meself, Tel. Honest.

**Terry**    Is that right?

**Alan**    Yeah, Tel, it's the trufe.

**Terry**    Maybe ya aint as fick as ya seem. Ere, Ficko, seein as yer bein honest fer once in yer life there's somefink I wanna ask ya. Where'd the name 'Goose' come frum?

**Alan**    Screw-loose.

**Terry**    I fuckin know that ya cunt. Ooh fort a the name Goose?

**Alan**    Dunno, Tel.

**Terry**    Ooh dya ear it frum then?

**Alan**    Can't remember off 'and, Tel.

**Terry** *picks up the knife from the table.*

**Terry**    Asked ya a question, Ficko. Wan an answer. Ooh was it?

**Alan**    Fink it was Dal I eard it frum, Tel.

**Terry** (*Raising his voice.*)    Dal! Ya fuckin eard it frum Dal?

**Alan**   Fink so, Tel.

**Terry**   An ooh'd e ear it frum?

**Alan**   I dunno mate. Onest. I dunno. Straight.

**Terry** *puts the knife on to the table and stands next to* **Alan**. *From his holdall he takes out some rope and ties* **Alan** *to the chair.*

**Alan**   What's appenin, Tel? Why ya tyin me up? Wotcha gonna do?

**Terry**   Ficko, no more talkin. Uv wivdrawn permission fer ya t' speak.

**Alan**   But I gotta tell ya. Please. It was . . .

**Terry** (*Interrupting.*)   Not annuver word, mate. An jus t' make sure . . .

**Terry** *takes a roll of parcel tape from his holdall and tapes* **Alan**'s *mouth shut. He snaps the end of the tape with his teeth.*

**Terry**   Jus nod yer ead yeah or shake yer ead no.

**Terry**   Dya know ooh Arvey Keitel is, Ficko?

**Alan** *shakes his head.*

**Terry**   E's a great actor e is, mate. I see im in *Bad Lieutenant* when I was sixteen. Me dad took me t' see it fer me birf-dee. Dal come wiv us. Geez in the box office wooden b'lieve we was eigh-een. Didn't wanna let us in. Me dad give im a score fer imself, an we was in. Arvey Keitel's a right nutter in it, a bent cozzer wiv a drug abit. Sure ya dun know ooh e is?

**Alan** *shakes his head.*

**Terry**   Ya earda the film *Reservoir Dogs*?

**Alan** *shakes his head.*

**Terry**   Well Arvey Keitel's in that, an when ya see *Reservoir Dogs* yul know ooh is cos e's the one ooh tries t' save Tim Roff. Ya know ooh Tim Roff is don'tcha?

**Alan** *shakes his head.*

**Terry**   Oh, fuck me mate ya dun know nuffink. Tim Roff's an English actor ooh made it big in Ollywood. Anyway, Arvey Keitel an Tim Roff stop this motor wiv a woman in cos they need a car t' escape see. Them an sum uvver mates ave jus nicked sum diamonds. An them two are tryin t' get away. So the woman's only got a shooter in the motor, aint she? An as Tim Roff opens the door the woman lets go a one. Roff's urt bad an Arvey Keitel elps im. They get t' this ware-ouse. Almost everyfink in the film appens in the ware-ouse. Then when Arvey Keitel finds out Roff's a cozzer e ends up finishin im off. An then e gets done imself.

**Terry** *stops talking, stares at* **Alan***, rubs his chin, nods and then starts talking again.*

**Terry**   I aint the type t' feel sympafy fer people ooh take me fer a mug, Ficko. But ya an me avin this little chat's set me finkin. Uv known Shall since we was young cos she ung round wiv me older sis. Did ya know that?

**Alan** *shakes his head.*

**Terry**   Well, when she got up the spout, when she was four-een wiv you, everyone was talkin bout it. Yer nan was never outa the boozer an Shall was nuffink but a troubled kid erself. S' ya was destined t' be fick. An though I feel jus the tiniest bit sorry fer ya mate I dun feel sorry nuff t' do nuffink. Cos then it gets round that people can ave me over easy. An I can't ave that. But I feel sorry nuff not t' urt ya *real* bad, jus bad nuff s' people know they can't take me fer no mug.

**Terry** *takes his phone from the table, taps the screen a couple of times and puts music on, places it back on the table. 'Stuck In The Middle With You', by Stealer's Wheel, starts playing at a just audible level.*

**Terry**   D'ya know this track, Ficko?

**Alan** *shakes his head.*

**Terry**　It's called 'Stuck In The Middle Wiv You'. It's by Stealer's Wheel. Ya dun know it?

**Alan** *shakes his head.*

**Terry**　It was used in the film I was jus tellin ya bout. It's one a me favourite tracks. I love it. Know all the words off by art I do. Ya aint never eard it?

**Alan** *shakes his head and* **Terry** *sings along to the track. He takes the razor-edge knife from the table and stands in front of* **Alan**.

**Terry**　No point even askin ya if ya know oo Michael Madsen is. Do ya know oo e is?

**Alan** *shakes his head.*

**Terry**　Course ya don't. Well t' all intents an purposes ya see me, um Michael Madsen, Mister cool. Mister fucking Blonde. Shirt an tie, smart an get fings done. (*Beat.*) That's me!

**Terry** *moves his body to the music and holding the knife in one hand he dances around and sings along. He dances to a position behind* **Alan** *and stands still. Pulling aside his hair, he slices clean through* **Alan**'s *left ear. Holding it gingerly he puts the ear on a shelf as* **Alan** *writhes.*

**Alan** (*In a stifled tone*)　Arrrrrrrrrgggggggggghhhhhhhh. Arrrrrrggggghhhhh.

**Terry** *takes a tissue from his pocket and wipes the knife. He puts the tissue in the pedal bin and puts the knife back down on to the table.*

**Terry**　Ya sound like a fuckin crow. Take the pain ya big girl. Done now. An if ya keep yer air long people might not even know it's missin.

**Terry** *waits a few seconds (singing along to some of the words) and then rips the tape off* **Alan**'s *mouth. He picks up his phone from the table and changes the music to random tracks and sets the volume to barely audible.*

**Terry**　There ya are, kiddo. Now ya can talk again. An ya got me permission t' speak. I fink ya oughta see the film.

**Alan** (*Almost crying.*)    I dunno wotcha talkin bout, Tel. Yuv cut me ear off. Yuv cut me fuckin ear off.

**Terry**    Not quite all uv left ya a bit. Um talkin bout *Reservoir Dogs*. I was jus tellin ya bout it. Wasn't ya list'nin?

**Alan** (*Sobbing.*)    Um in pain. Um fuckin urt.

**Terry**    Yer fuckin useless, that's wotcha'are. Listen. Arvey Keitel was Mister White. Tim Roff was Mister Orange. Then there's Mister Pink, Mister Brown, Mister Blue an a few uvvers. But Michael Madsen's me, Mister Blonde. Mister Blonde cut the cop's ear off. That's where I got the idea. Anyway, when ya see the film yul know what um talkin bout. An 'Stuck In The Middle Wiv You' yer always gonna remember. It'll be in yer ear-ole . . . I mean yer ead, forever. Ull get the dvd a the film fer ya sometime. A little prezzie. Ya got *any* money fer me, Ficko?

**Alan**    No, Tel. No I aint.

**Terry**    Ya aint got *no* money?

**Alan**    No, Tel. Straight. I aint.

**Terry**    Ya got gear then aintcha?

**Alan**    No, Tel, I aint.

**Terry**    Well that's a pity. Cos it means yer uvver ear's goin then init mate.

**Terry** *turns to reach for the knife.*

**Alan** (*Sobbing again.*)    No, no not me uvver ear as well, Tel. No. The gear's in me sock. It's in me sock, Tel.

**Terry** *leans down and removes a small plastic bag containing brown powder from* **Alan**'s *sock.* **Terry** *holds up the bag.*

**Terry**    Ow much ya got ere?

**Alan**    Bout six or so grams, Tel. Can't ya untie me arms so I can put somefink on me ear?

**Terry**   No, I can't. I aint decided what else t' do t' ya yet, Ficko. I told ya not t' make me come lookin fer ya. An I ain't sure one ear makes up fer ow much piss yuv taken outa me. S' ya got bout six gee's ere, eh. As it aint a proper quarter we'll say a two-ers worf. A straight bottle.

**Terry** *puts the bag of heroin into the inside pocket of his jacket.*

**Terry**   S' wiv the bottles worfa gear yuv kindly given me ere ya owe me a carpet right . . . right?

**Alan**   But yuv cut me ear off, Tel. That's gotta at least be worf a free-er. Wiv the quarter a gear yuv got can't we call it evens now?

**Terry**   As it appens I cut yer ear off fer late payment, lyin, an takin the piss outa me. But then it is jus possible ya got a point. Ya reckon that me cuttin yer ear off plus the bottles worfa gear means we should call it quits dya?

**Alan**   Yeah, Tel, that'd be fair.

**Terry**   It might be fair, though I aint positive bout that. But life's rarely fair, Ficko. I mean look at you.

**Rebecca** *walks in with the packet of Jaffa cakes.*

**Rebecca**   I ad t' go all the way down The Blue fer the Jaffa cakes.

**Rebecca** *stares to her left at* **Alan**, *tied up in the chair and softly sobbing.* **Alan**'s *missing left ear is not visible from where* **Rebecca** *is standing.*

**Rebecca**   Why's Al tied up? What's appened?

**Terry**   Gimme the Jaffa cakes please, Becks.

**Rebecca** *gives* **Terry** *the Jaffa cakes.*

**Terry**   Fanks. Any change frum the ching?

**Rebecca**   Yeah, ere.

**Rebecca** *hands* **Terry** *the change from the five-pound note and he puts it in his pocket. Then he opens the packet of cakes and holds it towards* **Rebecca**.

**Terry** Fanks. Dya want one?

**Rebecca** No fanks.

**Terry** *takes a Jaffa cake out and eats it.*

**Terry** Mmm, lovely them biscuits. Sit on the settee, Becks.

**Alan** Tel, can I ave a Jaffa cake?

**Terry** Ow many times I gotta tell ya? Where's yer fuckin manners?

**Alan** Please.

**Terry** Fer fuck's sake, ask proper.

**Alan** Can I ave a Jaffa cake, please Tel?

**Terry** *takes a Jaffa cake from the packet and puts it into* **Alan**'s *mouth.* **Rebecca** *sits on the settee and she sees the knife on the table. But with* **Alan**'s *hair being long, she still can't see that his ear is missing.*

**Terry** Ere, Becks. Ya know the film *Reservoir Dogs* don'tcha?

**Rebecca** Yeah, it's me mum's favourite film. She's got it on dvd.

**Terry** Great. Ya watched it recent?

**Rebecca** What's happenin ere, Tel? Whats goin on? Why's Al tied up?

**Terry** I ate people not answerin me questions. Can ya answer or not?

**Rebecca** Um not concentratin. What was the question?

**Terry** I asked ya wever yuv watched *Reservoir Dogs* recent?

**Rebecca**   Not that recent but recent nuff t' remember it.

**Terry**   Dya know that Ficko dun even know ooh Tim Roff is. Ya know ooh Tim Roff is don'tcha?

**Rebecca**   Yeah course I do. E's in *Reservoir Dogs*. E's frum Deptford.

**Terry**   E's in *Reservoir Dogs* but e aint frum Deptford. E's frum Dulwich.

**Rebecca**   Um sure e's frum Deptford, Tel.

**Terry**   Listen, I know where e's frum an it aint Deptford. Maybe e did is shoppin in Deptford. But e's frum fuckin Dulwich.

**Rebecca**   Ok Tel, I got it wrong then.

**Alan**   E's cut me ear off, Becks. E's only cut me fuckin ear off . . .

**Rebecca**   (*Sounding incredulous.*)   Yuv cut is ear off, Tel? I can't believe yuv cut is ear off.

**Terry**   Ere, Becks, listen t' this track.

**Rebecca**   What!?

**Terry**   Jus listen.

**Terry** *takes his phone from the table and holding it in his hand he puts 'Stuck In The Middle With You' on. Holding the phone he moves his body and sings along.*

**Terry**   Dya remember the bit frum the film where this track was playin? The scene wiv Michael Madsen, Mister Blonde?

**Rebecca**   Yeah, Tel, I remember it.

**Terry**   'Course ya do, great scene, great track.

**Terry** *turns the track off and puts random music back on with the volume barely audible. He puts his phone back down on the table.*

**Rebecca**    But that's in a film, Tel. I can't believe yuv actually cut Al's ear off.

**Alan**    Becks, Becks, untie me. I gotta get t' the ospital.

**Rebecca**    Untie im frum the chair, Tel. Let im do somefink.

**Terry**    Wotcha talkin bout? Let im do what?

**Rebecca**    Dunno. Maybe they can sew is ear back on if e goes t' ospital.

**Terry**    E aint gettin outa that chair fer awhile yet, Becks. As it goes can ya take is ear off the shelf an chuck it out the winda. Fuckin fing's givin me earache.

**Rebecca**    That jus aint funny, Tel. I aint doin it. It's disgustin, it is.

**Terry** *walks over and picks the ear up from the shelf and then holds it up in front of his eyes.*

**Terry**    Bout disgustin. Ull tell ya what's disgustin. I'm not payin . . . (**Terry** *looks closely at the ear.*) Ere ang on. Can ya Adam an Eve it? Fuck me. Look Becks. Al's got a tiny little stud in the top of is ear. It's that small I never noticed it.

**Rebecca**    As e Tel?

**Terry**    Yeah e, as. Look, can'tcha see it?

**Terry** *holds the ear towards* **Rebecca**.

**Rebecca**    Yeah, Tel just about. But ud sooner not look.

**Terry**    If ud noticed it ud ave cut is uvver ear off. Ficko, ya got a stud in the ear ya got left.

**Alan**    No.

**Terry**    Ya could get yer uvver one pierced an put this stud in that one. Wadya reckon?

**Alan**    Ud sooner get that ear stitched back on, Tel. The one wiv the stud in.

**Terry**   I betcha wood. But yuv lied an taken the piss outa me. An ya never paid me back me money. If ya got yer ear stitched back on ya wooden ave ad no punishment.

**Alan**   Course I wood, Tel. Yuv cut me ear off. Even if it's stitched back on it's gonna leave a psychology scar.

**Terry**   I fink ya mean a psychological scar.

**Alan**   Whatever, Tel, it's gonna leave one.

**Terry**   Yeah, it is gonna leave one. An maybe it'll make ya fink twice before lyin an lendin readies an not payin them readies back. Sorry, can't take the stud out yer ear mate. Bit too messy. Becks, dya wanna take the stud out is ear before I chuck it?

**Rebecca**   No.

**Terry** *picks the ear up and stands next to the window.*

**Terry**   *Ear* goes.

*He drops the ear out of the window.*

**Terry**   Now that were funny, weren't it?

**Rebecca**   No it weren't. Ya need elp, Tel.

**Terry**   Wotcha goin on bout (*Beat.*) (*shouting*) I need elp. (**Terry** *stops talking and he looks up at the ceiling. His face contorts, then relaxes and he starts talking with his voice slightly raised.*) Ya moufey bitch. Ya bin sayin bad fings bout me.

**Rebecca**   No, Tel, I aint.

**Terry**   Oh yeah ya ave. Siddown over there.

**Terry** *points to the other chair.*

**Rebecca**   I wanna go now, Tel. Please lemme go.

**Terry**   Ull only ask ya one more time, Becks. Dun fuck wiv me. Siddown there.

**Terry** *points again to the other chair.* **Rebecca** *moves the other chair next to* **Alan** *and sits down on it.*

**Rebecca**    Now what Tel. Ya gonna cut me ear off too?

**Terry**    Shut up an keep quiet while I fink.

**Terry** *rubs his chin. Pause.*

**Alan**    Please, Tel. Lemme get sum elp.

**Terry** *shakes his head as if to clear his thoughts.*

**Terry**    What?

**Alan**    I could bleed t' deff, Tel.

**Terry**    That'd be a result. Get sum toilet paper, Becks, an dab where is ear should be.

**Alan**    I aint got no toilet paper.

**Terry**    Dya ear that, Becks? E aint got no fuckin bog roll. Wadya do? Use yer fuckin and t' wipe yer arse? Find a t-shirt or somefink fer im.

**Rebecca** *exits the lounge and goes into the bedroom. She re-enters holding a pale grey t-shirt.*

**Alan**    Oh no, not that one. That's me Frank Sinatra.

**Rebecca**    What!! Yer worried bout what t-shirt um gonna use?

**Alan**    That's me favourite.

**Terry**    Fuckin Frank Sinatra. Ere, open that t-shirt out, Becks.

**Rebecca** *holds up the t-shirt. On the front is a picture of Frank Sinatra and underneath the picture, the words, 'Frank Sinatra, A Legend'.*

**Terry**    'Frank Sinatra, A fuckin Legend'. Ere, Ficko, where the fuck dya get that t-shirt?

**Alan**    One a the ol Turks gimme it.

**Terry**   Dya even know ooh Frank Sinatra is?

**Alan**   No Tel, I jus like the t-shirt. Ooh is e?

**Terry**   E was President of the United States, mate.

**Alan**   Was e? I never knew that. Ya aint gonna do nuffink more t' me are ya? Yuv punished me nuff by cuttin me ear off. An jus fer a monkey.

**Terry**   That's right. Jus fer a fuckin monkey. But also cos yer such a lyin, cheatin, big mouf cunt. Fuckin 'Goose' . . . liber-ee. Oh, an uv bin finkin bout wotcha said. Ya reckoned yer ear was worf a carpet didn'tcha?

**Alan**   Yeah, Tel.

**Rebecca**   Lemme untie im, Tel. What's the matter wiv ya? Ya aint gonna torture im no more are ya?

**Terry** (*Raised voice.*)   Jus siddown in the fuckin armchair.

**Rebecca**   Can't I stay ere, Tel? Then I can dab the blood on Al's ear.

**Terry** (*Raised, threatening voice.*)   Move, sit in the fuckin armchair.

**Rebecca**   No Tel. Um ok ere in this chair. Ya asked me t' sit ere.

**Terry**   That was then. This is now. Stop dabbin where is fuckin ear should be. An do like I tell ya. Sit in the fuckin armchair.

**Rebecca**   Why, Tel?

**Terry** (*Raised, threatening voice.*)   Jus sit in the fuckin armchair *now*, will ya?

**Rebecca**   Ok, ok Tel. Um gonna sit in the armchair. But please dun do nuffink t' me. Please, Tel. We're mates, Tel. We're mates.

**Terry**   Jus shut yer mouf an move.

**Rebecca** *gets up from the chair and as she sidles past the table* **Alan** *speaks.*

**Alan**    Please untie me, Tel. It was Dal fort a the name 'Goose'. Onest, it was. Please dun do nuffink else, Tel.

*Hearing that,* **Terry** *is distracted and* **Rebecca** *manages to pick up the knife from the table. She sits in the armchair with her arm dangling over the side holding the knife.*

**Terry**    Dal made up that name?

**Alan**    Yeah Tel.

**Terry**    Becks, did Dal gimme the nickname, 'Goose'?

**Rebecca**    Not that I know of Tel. I aint never even eard that name before.

**Alan**    It's true, Tel. E did. E did.

**Terry**    Right, that's it. Shut it now. Uv wivdrawn permission fer ya t' speak.

**Terry** *stands in front of the armchair.*

**Terry**    Fuckin buncha losers. An you, yuv bin talkin bad bout me. Aintcha Becks? Betcha bin callin me Goose as well.

**Rebecca**    I aint, Tel. I aint never eard that name before. I never say nuffink bad boutcha Tel.

**Terry**    Dun lie t' me Becks.

**Rebecca**    I aint lyin, Tel. I aint never said nuffink bad boutcha. Honest.

**Terry**    Skirts an igh eels, eh? Ud like ya dressin up fer me like that.

**Rebecca**    Tel, untie Al an lemme go. Yuv taught Al is lesson. Dun do nuffink else Tel.

**Terry**    Ya fink I dunno. But I do see.

**Rebecca**    Wotcha talkin bout, Tel?

**Terry**   Ya bin bad moufin me. (*And raising his voice.*) Fer no fuckin good reason. Aintcha?

**Rebecca** (*Almost crying.*)   No, no I aint Tel. Tel, Tel, ya got it wrong. Tel, ya got it wrong.

**Terry** (*Screaming.*)   Shut up, shut up . . .

**Terry** *looks up, his face contorts and he stays like that for a couple of seconds. Then he puts his hands round* **Rebecca**'s *throat and tightens them.*

**Rebecca**   No Tel . . . Tel . . . nooooooooo, noooooooooooo.

**Rebecca** *lifts her hand with the knife in but* **Terry** *grabs her wrist and forces her to drop the knife from her hand. He again starts strangling* **Rebecca** *but then suddenly stops and, collapsing on to the settee, he stares transfixed at the ceiling. Slowly* **Rebecca** *gets up holding her throat. She takes the half-filled Coke off the table and drinks from it.*

**Rebecca** (*Coughing.*)   Tel, Tel . . . can I untie Al?

**Terry** *doesn't answer.*

**Rebecca**   Tel, ya ok?

*Pause.*

**Rebecca**   Tel, ya ok mate? Ya look a bit green.

**Terry** *stops staring at the ceiling. He shakes his head and then looks at Becks.*

**Terry**   What?

**Rebecca**   Ya alright Tel?

**Terry**   Was feelin a bit queasy there. Come to now though. Um real sorry, Becks. Real sorry. Ya ok?

**Rebecca**   Yeah Tel. Bit of a sore froat. But um ok.

**Terry**   Dunno why I done it. Them fuckin lousies gimme a visit an . . .

**Rebecca** (*Interrupting.*)    Them what?

**Terry**    Them lousies, them whispers. Dunno where they come frum.

**Rebecca**    Whispers? Right. Can I untie Al?

**Terry**    Yeah.

**Rebecca** *unties* **Alan**.

**Alan**    Alright if I go look fer me ear, Tel?

**Terry**    Fuck off cunt.

**Alan** *picks up the Frank Sinatra t-shirt and, holding it to the side of his head, he walks towards the door but then stops and turns to* **Rebecca**.

**Alan**    Ya wanna elp me look fer me ear, Becks?

**Rebecca**    Nah, I don't.

**Alan** *exits*.

**Rebecca**    Um goin to me mum's. See ya Tel.

**Terry**    Yeah, ok. I dunno what t' say Becks. But ya know um real sorry.

**Rebecca**    Yeah, I know, Tel, I know.

**Terry**    Maybe I could make up fer it. Bring ya a few Juicies. Size small. Ow bout it?

**Rebecca**    Yeah sure. Give it a cupla weeks though. Um gonna stay at me mum's fer a bit. Feel I need a break frum the block. See ya.

**Terry**    Yeah, see ya girl.

**Rebecca** *exits*.

**Terry** *remains sitting on the settee and he leans forward to turn the music a little louder. He moves his body along with the music. Six seconds pass with the sound of the lift just audible. Then five seconds later* **Alan**'s *voice penetrates the open window.*

**Alan**  Yay . . . yay, uv found me ear. Uv found me ear . . .

**Terry** *looks towards the window with a wide-eyed expression. Running over, he looks out and shouts.*

**Terry**  Oyyyyyyyy Ficko. Oyyyyy. (*He walks away from the window and mutters out loud to himself.*) Dun even answer, ignorant fuck.

**Terry** *takes his phone off the table and changes the music. 'The Needle And The Damage Done', by Neil Young, starts playing. He takes off his jacket and from the holdall he takes out a syringe filled with brown liquid. As he sings along to the track he rolls up his shirt sleeve, removes the cap on the syringe, puts it on the table and injects himself. After withdrawing the needle he dabs his arm with a tissue from his pocket. He puts the cap back on the empty syringe and throws it along with the tissue in the pedal bin. Rolling down his sleeve he puts his jacket back on and sits down on the settee singing along. Three seconds pass and there is a knock on the door. Startled,* **Terry** *stands and calls out.*

**Terry**  Ooh is it?

**Darren**  Is that ya Tel?

**Terry**  Yeah it fuckin is.

**Darren** *walks in and* **Terry** *picks up his phone from the table, turns the music off and places his mobile back where it was.*

**Darren**  'iya Tel.

**Terry**  Jus the person I wanna see.

**Darren**  Yeah?

**Terry**  Yeah, Dal. We need t' ave a little chat, ya an me.

**Darren**  Sure Tel.

**Terry** *sits on the settee and* **Darren** *goes to sit next to him.*

**Terry**  Sit in the armchair Dal.

**Darren**  But I always sit on the settee when um up ere, Tel.

**Terry**    Do ya?

**Darren**    Yeah, always.

**Terry**    Well yer gonna ave t' change yer abits aintcha? Cos this time yer gonna sit in the armchair.

**Darren**    Okay Tel. No prob. Armchair it is, mate. Ere, can I ave one of them Jaffa cakes?

**Terry**    Is that ow ya always ask?

**Darren**    Oh, sorry Tel, meant t' say please.

**Terry**    Yeah, well ok. Spose ya can.

**Darren** *sits in the armchair. He leans forward and picks up the packet of Jaffa cakes and takes one out and eats it.* **Terry** *leans forward and takes out a Jaffa cake and talks as he eats it.*

**Terry**    We've got some serious stuff t' sort out, ya an me mate. But first uv got sumfink on me mind an I need to ask ya a question.

**Darren**    Yeah, course, ask away mate.

**Terry**    Wadya do wiv yer used works?

**Darren**    Me used works!!?

**Terry**    Is it a difficult question? (*And spoken slowly.*) Wadya do wiv yer needles after yuv ad an it?

**Darren**    I frow em in the sharps bin, Tel.

**Terry**    Oh right, ok. S' ya aint never frown em out the winda?

**Darren**    No, never.

**Terry**    An what bout Jack an Sam?

**Darren**    They aint fixers, they only chase.

**Terry**    That lyin fuck.

**Darren**    Wotcha talkin bout, Tel?

**Terry**   Dun matter.

**Terry** *stares at* **Dal** *and rubs his chin and nods his head.*

**Terry**   Ere Dal, dya remember when we went wiv me dad t' see *Bad Lieutenant* fer me sixteenf?

**Darren**   Oh yeah, yeah. I do mate. Fuckin ell. That's a few years back init? Ooh was in that again?

**Terry**   Arvey Keitel, mate. E was the fucked-up cozzer.

**Darren**   Was e? Can't remember that.

**Terry**   Arvey Keitel frum *Reservoir Dogs*.

**Darren**   Yeah, I know ooh Arvey Keitel is. I know e's in *Reservoir Dogs*. But I was only a kid when we see *Bad Lieutenant*, can't remember im in that. Can't even remember ooh's in *Reservoir Dogs*. Oh yeah, ang on, I fink I do. It's Tim Roff init?

**Terry**   Yeah that's right. Becks fort e was frum Deptford?

**Darren**   E is frum Deptford.

**Terry**   What is it wiv Tim Roff an Deptford. E aint frum fuckin Deptford. E's frum fuckin Dulwich.

**Darren**   Alright, Tel. I jus fort e was frum Deptford that's all.

**Terry**   Well e aint, alright?

**Darren**   Yeah Tel, alright. (*Beat.*) They bofe start wiv 'D' though dun they?

**Terry**   Wotcha talkin bout, Dal? They bofe start wiv 'D'?

**Darren**   Well, like ya know. Dulwich starts wiv a 'D' an so does Deptford.

**Terry**   What the fuck's that got t' do wiv anyfink? I jus dunno where yer finkin comes frum. I fink ya got a touch a the Aspergers mate.

**Darren**    Oh, dun say that Tel. Everyone down the Social's got that. Ya fink I gotit?

**Terry**    Dal, there aint nuffink wrong wiv ya mate, yer jus a bit slow that's all.

**Darren**    Slow. Ya reckon um slow, Tel?

**Terry**    Yeah slow, but ya got a sorta . . . a sorta honesty boutcha. I like that. Ya can't be no one but yerself. Whereas me, mosta the time I aint gotta clue ooh I am. It's ard sometimes. Dya know what I mean, Dal?

*As* **Darren** *goes to answer he looks around and sees the rope on the floor.*

**Darren**    Well . . . ere, ang on Tel, there's rope on the floor there mate.

**Terry**    Ya aint even list'nin t' me. I ate people not answerin me questions.

**Darren**    Yeah, Tel, I am. I know wotcha mean mate. I know. But it's strange that rope bein on the floor init?

**Terry**    Per'aps Ficko's bin indulgin in a bita bondage stuff, eh?

**Darren**    Bondage. Ficko, bondage!? Wooden even like t' imagine it mate. Ya reckon e's a prevert?

**Terry**    A what?

**Darren**    A prevert, ya know. Someone oo's a bit fucked up in the sexual department like.

**Terry**    It's fuckin pervert not fuckin prevert.

**Darren**    Oh yeah, yeah. Always get them two mixed up. Ere Tel, I was jus sittin in me front room an I eard Ficko shoutin frum downstairs that e'd found is ear. When I looked out e was doin the undred-yard sprint out the estate. What's e talkin bout, Tel?

**Terry**   Wadya fink e's talkin bout? E lost is ear an now e's found it. Simple.

**Darren**   Dunno wotcha mean, Tel. I aint wiv ya. Ya dun jus lose yer ear. It dun jus drop off. I mean, it aint like a dog an bone or somefink, falls out yer pocket.

**Terry**   Fer fuck's sake, Dal. E lost is ear cos I cut it off. That's ow e fuckin lost it.

**Darren**   Fuckin ell, Tel. Ya cut Ficko's ear off!? That's severe init mate?

**Terry**   E ad t' be taught a lesson.

**Darren**   Arsh lesson though init? Fuckin ell, that's grim mate. Which ear dya cut off, Tel?

**Terry**   Does it matter?

**Darren**   Well e ad a stud in one, that's all. Unusual cos it's tiny an it's right at the top of is ear.

**Terry**   What bout it then?

**Darren**   Well that's why um askin which ear.

**Terry**   If ya mus know it was is fuckin left ear. The one wiv the stud in.

**Darren**   Bit of a shame that, Tel. E's ad that stud in since he were five. Ya know Shall was jus a kid. An Ficko told me she done is ear wiva sewin needle fer is fiff birf-dee. His nan got im the stud an e aint never took it out since. Not that e's sentimental, Ficko, but that stud's bout the only close connection e's got to is ma an is nan.

**Terry**   Social work.

**Darren**   What Tel?

**Terry**   Social work. Forget feevin. That's what ya need t' be doin Dal, social fuckin work. Well Ficko's family connection's presently *detached* aint it? Anyway, e's found is ear now aint e? An the stud's still in it. If e gets it sewn on e'll be reconnected won't e? Ere, Dal, yer meant t' be me mate ain'tcha?

**Darren**   I am yer mate, Tel. But that dun mean I can't ave me own opinion. I still fink it was arsh cuttin Ficko's ear off.

**Terry**   Do ya? Well as it goes I weren't talkin bout that. I was talkin bout somefink serious. But anyway, *ya* deal wiv fings ow ya wanna deal wiv em. An ull deal wiv em ow I wanna deal wiv em. Alright?

**Darren**   Yeah alright Tel. Was Becks up ere?

**Terry**   Yeah she was. We ad a bit of a bull an cow. Fink she was a bit put out when I asked er t' chuck Ficko's ear out the winda. She's gone t' er mum's. Ere Dal, I was right pissed off wiv ya, I can tell ya. I mean more than jus really pissed off wiv ya. I was really, really really pissed off wiv ya. No word of a lie. I was that wound up I was gonna knock ya out soon as I see ya mate. But I ad an it, an it calmed me down a bit. Dya know why I was that pissed off wiv ya Dal? (*And raising his voice.*) Ya got any clue?

**Darren**   No Tel. I aint gotta clue.

**Terry**   Well there's somefink I wanna ask ya.

**Darren**   Ask away.

**Terry**   Ya eaten any Duck lately mate?

**Darren** (*In a surprised voice.*)   Wadya say, Tel?

**Terry**   Ya Mutt an Jeff or what?

**Darren**   No I aint. But I dunno wever I caught it right. Did ya ask me if ud eaten any Duck lately?

**Terry**   Yeah that's right. I did. An ave ya?

**Darren**   I ave as it appens. Ad some last week frum the Chinese.

**Terry**   Yeah, didya? An does the Chinese sell fuckin Goose?

**Darren**   Oh no. Oh no Tel. I can't b'lieve it mate. Ficko an is big fuckin mouf.

**Terry**   Yeah Ficko an is big fuckin mouf. The ole a Souf London's callin me Goose now. Fanks t' you.

**Darren**   I only meant it as a joke, Tel. It was jus a joke mate. Honest. I never wanted it t' go nowhere. Serious, Tel, I never.

*As* **Darren** *fidgets awkwardly he looks down and sees the knife on the floor.*

**Darren**   Ere Tel, there's a blade on the floor mate.

**Terry**   Pick it up then.

**Darren** *picks the knife up and hands it towards* **Terry**.

**Terry**   Perhaps ya should ang on t' it mate. Ya might need it.

**Darren**   I aint a blade kinda person. I aint the violent type. Ya know that.

*Leaning forwards,* **Darren** *puts the knife on the table.*

**Terry**   Yeah I know that. Yuv got sum bottle puttin that blade down in fronta me like that. Ya ave, ya really ave. Straight up. Specially after inventin a name like that. An in fronta Ficko. But it shows ow well ya know me, Dal.

**Terry** *stops talking, looks at* **Darren** *and rubs his chin.*

**Terry**   We've bin froo loads t'gever ya an me mate. Life's built on memories. An all the good memories I got ya was there.

**Darren**   Same fer me init, Tel. Ya an me bin friends since infants at St Joseph's. Then right froo St Michael's. Seems like we known each uvver forever.

**Terry**   Yeah, fuckin ell. Even walkin t' school t'gever. Fuck. I aint got *no* uvver real mates. No one ooh goes back as far as ya an me. The mates ya make when yer young ya can never make again.

**Darren**   That's true Tel, yeah. We go way back.

**Terry**   I wanna, I tell ya . . . but ow the fuck can I urt ya?

**Darren**   Tel listen. I made a mistake, mate. Plain an simple. Ud never take the piss outa ya. I was outa me ead an I was jus finkin out loud. Ficko appened t' be wiv me. Um right sorry I fort up that name, Tel. I am mate. Honest, I am.

**Terry**   Did Becks know ya invented that name?

**Darren**   Yeah she did. I told er bout it. Said I made a right mistake inventin it in fronta Ficko.

**Terry**   She told me she never eard it before. Stuck up fer ya. She's rare er, real rare. Fuckin loyal. Yeah, one a yer own, mate.

**Darren**   Yeah she is. One a yer own. I know.

**Terry**   Yeah she's a bit special alright, er. Ya know Dal, I weren't even gonna talk. I was jus gonna knock ya sparko. No questions asked. But as it goes the more I fink bout it the more um gettin used t' it. Goose. Aint terrible is it? Long as no one says it t' me face cos then they'll get urt. An I spose it coulda bin worse.

**Darren**   Phew! Um real relieved bout that Tel. Straight, I am. Right relieved. An it coulda bin worse. Yer right. It *coulda* bin Duck. Though when I was out me ead finkin a names I never fort a that one.

**Terry**   Wotcha talkin bout Dal, Duck?

**Darren**   Well it coulda bin like ya know . . . mad fuck . . . Duck. Goose is better than Duck init?

**Terry**   Mad Fuck!? Are ya tryin t' wind me up, Dal?

**Darren**   No Tel, no. No I aint. Um jus sayin that's all.

**Terry**   Fuckin Duck!

**Darren**   Sorry Tel, jus finkin out loud again. That's all. Ya know what um like, mate.

**Terry**   Yeah I know wotcha like but I tell ya. Sometimes ya really push yer luck wiv me mate. Fuckin ell. Yer jus lucky I know ya s' well. An that's why yer the only one I can ask.

**Darren**   Ask what, Tel?

**Terry**   Well it's sorta sensitive like. That's why I wanna know what ya fink. Man t' man like.

**Darren**   It's alright Tel, ask away mate.

**Terry**   Well I told ya me an Becks ad a little sorta, run-in sorta fing. I sorta lost it wiv er a bit. Them lousies paid me a visit. Started finkin weird fings an I sorta lost it a bit.

**Darren**   Oh no, what appened. She alright?

**Terry** (*Raising his voice.*)   Yeah course she's alright. Bit of a sore froat she reckoned. But part frum that she's sweet as.

**Darren**   That's good then. Though she never ad a sore froat last night. Was talkin like a goodun.

**Terry**   Yeah well, see, I strangled er a bit. That's what appened.

**Darren**   Oh no, fuck. She's alright though?

**Terry**   Yeah I jus told ya she's sweet as. Aintcha list'nin?

**Darren**   Yeah Tel, I am. I am. What was it ya wanted t' ask me. Man t' man like.

**Terry**   Dya fink uv blown me chances wiv Becks? That's what I wanted t' ask ya.

**Darren** (*Sounding surprised and raising his voice.*)   What's that Tel?

**Terry**   Are ya goin fuckin deaf or what? Um askin ya wever ya fink uv blown me chances wiv Becks?

**Darren**   Errrr . . . errrr . . . I, I dunno mate. I errr . . . dunno. Honest I jus dunno.

**Terry**   Wadya fink?

**Darren**    I dunno Tel. Um sorta shocked yer askin me, mate. I aint really the right person t' ask fer advice bout that sorta fing.

**Terry**    Dal, um askin ya what ya fink. Are ya gonna tell me?

**Darren**    Honest, Tel. I jus aint good at that advice stuff mate.

**Terry**    A cupla minutes back ya said ya ad yer own opinion.

**Darren**    I ave got me own opinion. But that dun mean um good at givin advice on what women fink.

**Terry**    Fuckin ell, mate. Um only askin ya man t' man what ya fink. Um still in wiv a chance wiv er aint I? Come on, sum advice mate. I aint gonna old it gainst ya, am I?

**Darren**    Well Tel, what I fink, mate, like t' be honest like. If ya fancy someone it probly aint the best idea cuttin their mate's ear off. An then askin em t' frow that mate's ear out the winda, well . . . ? (*Beat*.) An then tryin t' strangle em? Um not sure that would make the best impression like. (*Pause – then nodding his head.*) Know what I mean, Tel?

**Terry** *fixes a stare at* **Darren** *and leans forward. Pointing his finger and moving it up down,* **Terry** *speaks.*

**Terry**    Ya know yer problem, Dal, yer too much of a pessimist mate. Ya only see the blocks, where me, I see the reds.

**Darren**    Dunno wotcha mean, Tel, what the fuck's the blocks an the reds?

**Terry**    The blocks are the block sinuses, the minuses mate. An the reds are the red buses, the pluses. Alright!?

**Darren**    Alright, Tel, alright. Cupla yours are they those?

**Terry**    Yeah mate.

**Darren**    Well fort out. The red buses, the pluses. The block sinuses, the minuses.

**Terry**   Exactly. An where I see the fuckin red buses ya see the block sinuses.

**Darren**   Ya fink?

**Terry**   Yeah I do. An I can tell ya Becks is well impressed wiv me. Wadya reckon?

**Darren**   Well . . . erhh, um . . .

**Terry**   The reds, Dal, the pluses, mate, the pluses.

**Darren**   'Course, Tel, yeah. Dunno why I can't see them reds.

**Terry**   That's ya all over, Dal. Ya gotta start focusin on the reds mate.

**Darren**   I'll work on it, Tel.

**Terry**   Ya know what Dal?

**Darren**   What's that Tel?

**Terry**   The little sorta fing goin on wiv me an Becks gotta be followed up on aint it?

**Darren**   Well, errrhh . . .

**Terry**   The reds mate. Stick t' the fuckin red buses.

**Darren**   Yeah course, dunno what um doin. Finkin bout the blocks. The reds yeah. Yeah, 'course ya gotta follow up, yeah deffo.

**Terry**   Might even pop round to er mum's place. Aint seen er ma in years. Wadya reckon?

**Darren**   Errrhh . . .

**Terry**   The red buses, Dal, finka the reds.

**Darren**   Yeah Tel, I am mate.

**Terry**   Good. Wadya fink bout me goin round Becks's ma's t' visit er then?

**Darren**   Yep. Great idea, Tel. Maybe give it a cupla days eh?

**Terry**   Yeah, yeah. Good advice mate. Cupla days yeah. S' wiv fings the way they are. Looks like I could be back t' doin a bita biz in me ol patch. Bermondsey beckons. Wadya fink?

**Darren**   Mmm, yeah, yeah . . . sounds good mate.

**Terry**   Does. Fink yul be seein me real soon me ol fruitgum.

*Pause.*

**Darren**   Great Tel, great . . .

*Lights dim, act closes.*

*End.*

**Glossary**

*Monetary terms*

| | | |
|---|---|---|
| Ching | = | £5.00 |
| Cockle | = | £10.00 |
| Score | = | £20.00 |
| Bullseye | = | £50.00 |
| Longun | = | £100.00 |
| Bottle | = | £200.00 |
| Carpet | = | £300.00 |
| Monkey | = | £500.00 |

*Drug terms*

| | | |
|---|---|---|
| Brown | = | heroin |
| Chase | = | As in 'chasing the dragon'. Taking heroin by burning it on silver foil. |
| Gear | = | heroin |
| Joey | = | £10.00 deal |
| Meff | = | Methadone |
| Rock | = | crack cocaine |
| Sniff | = | cocaine powder |
| Works | = | hypodermic syringe |

*Others*

| | | |
|---|---|---|
| Adam and Eve | = | believe |
| bull and cow | = | row |
| clobber | = | clothes |
| daisy roots | = | daisies = boots |
| dog and bone | = | phone |
| drum | = | house/flat |
| drummer | = | burglar |
| moody | = | fake |
| mutt and jeff | = | deaf |
| railings | = | teeth |
| term | = | jail sentence |
| tourni | = | tourniquet |